Cobblestone Cats

Miraflores

Lima

Panattoni

www.panattoniprintshop.com

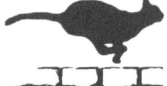

Cobblestone Cats

Cats of Miraflores

Lima is the capital of Peru and it is big and busy with a population of almost 10 million people. It offers tasty Peruvian cuisine, long beach fronts, and beautiful green parks. One of these parks is Parque Kennedy located in the heart of Miraflores, one of Lima's main districts. Parque Kennedy occupies an area of approximately 240,000 square feet and was named in honor of President Kennedy for the aid he provided Peru during his presidency. In the park you can find everything from artisans, street food vendors, locals and tourist, beautifully manicured flowerbeds and of course cats.

As the story goes, the first two cats were introduced 25 years ago by a priest from a Catholic Church located alongside the park grounds. Now, the park is populated by dozens of cats, some domestic and friendly and others feral and street tuff. The cats of Miraflores hangout like a local taking a stroll, you will see cats at foot asking for a bit of someones lunch, taking a nap on a tourist lap, perched in a tree, or peeking up and out of a flowerbed. A group of dedicated volunteers, Gatos Kennedy Oficial, care for the cats and will trap, neuter and release to help control the cat population. They also find homes for the cats through their adoption program.

The Cats of Miraflores are documented through these pages . . . .

.... Enjoy!

The ancestor of all domestic cats is the African Wild Cat which still exists today

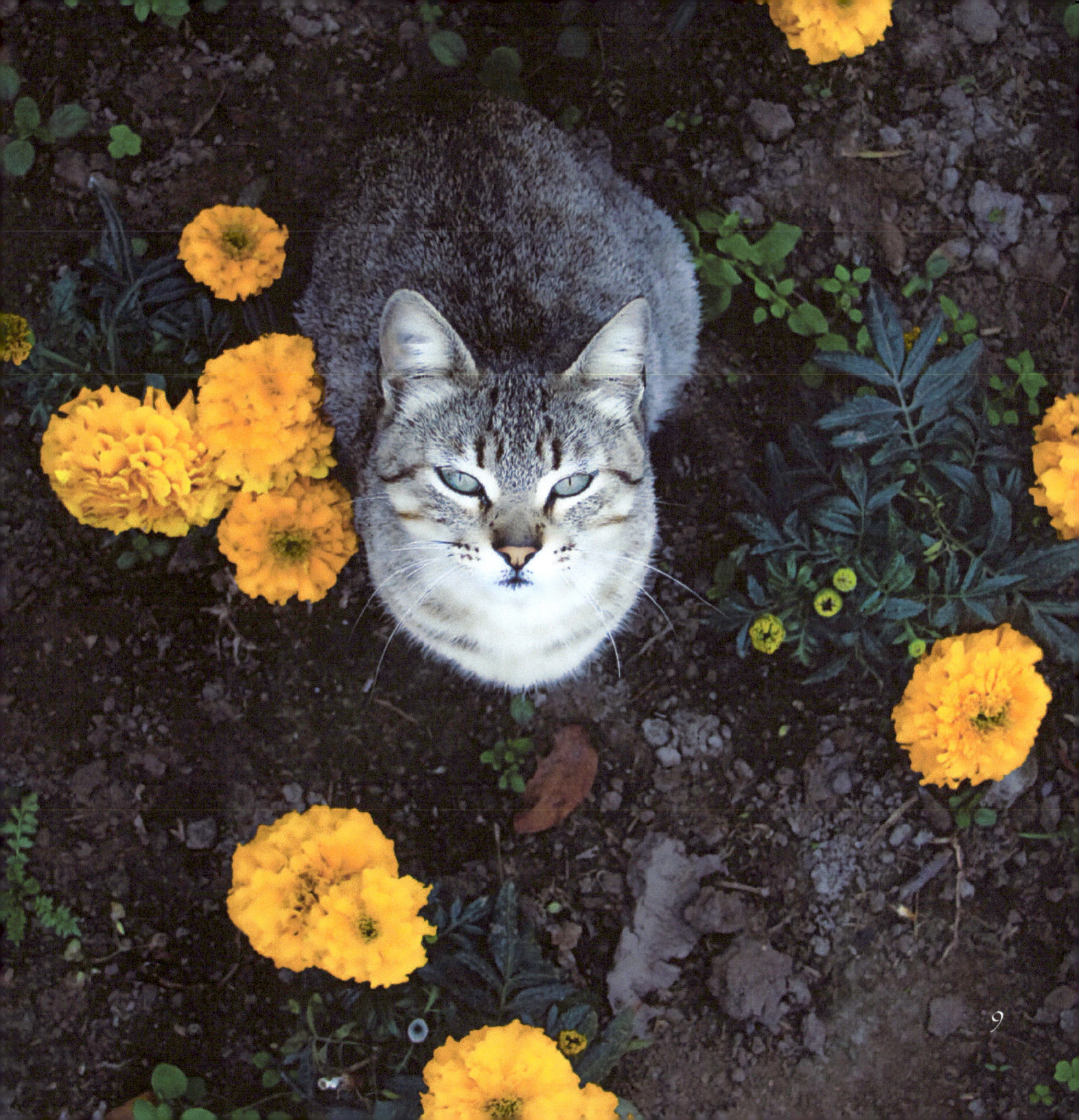

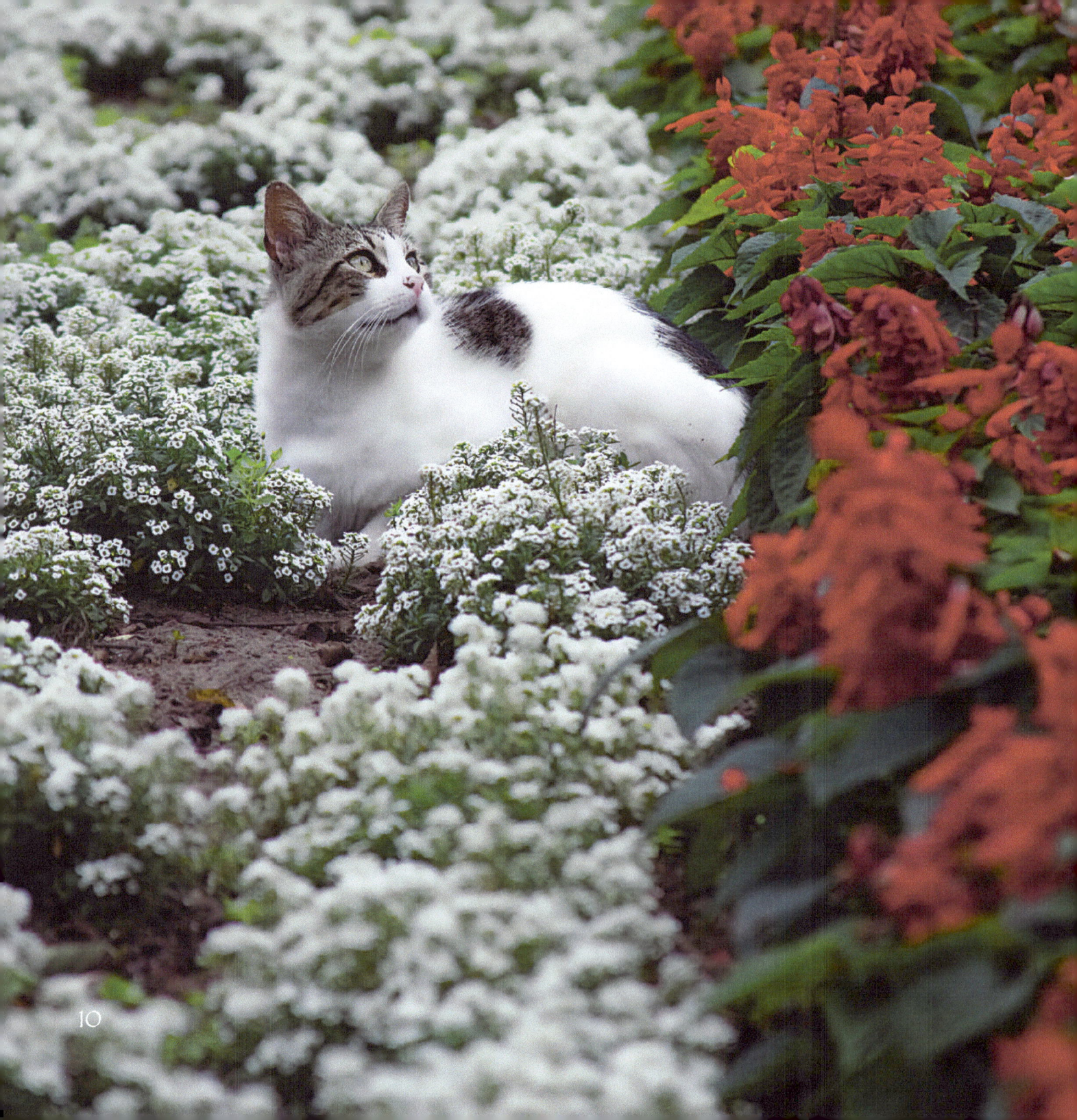

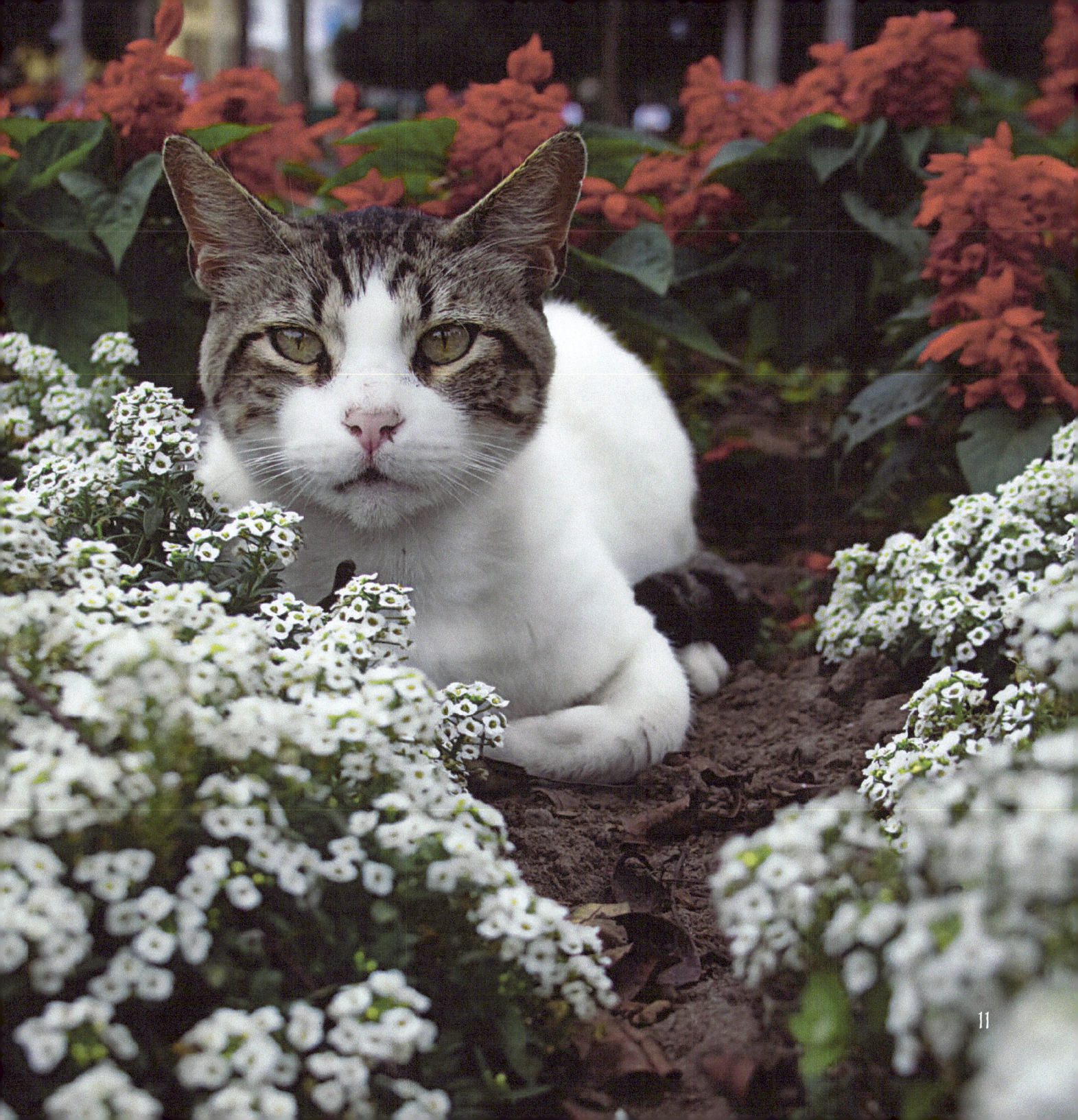

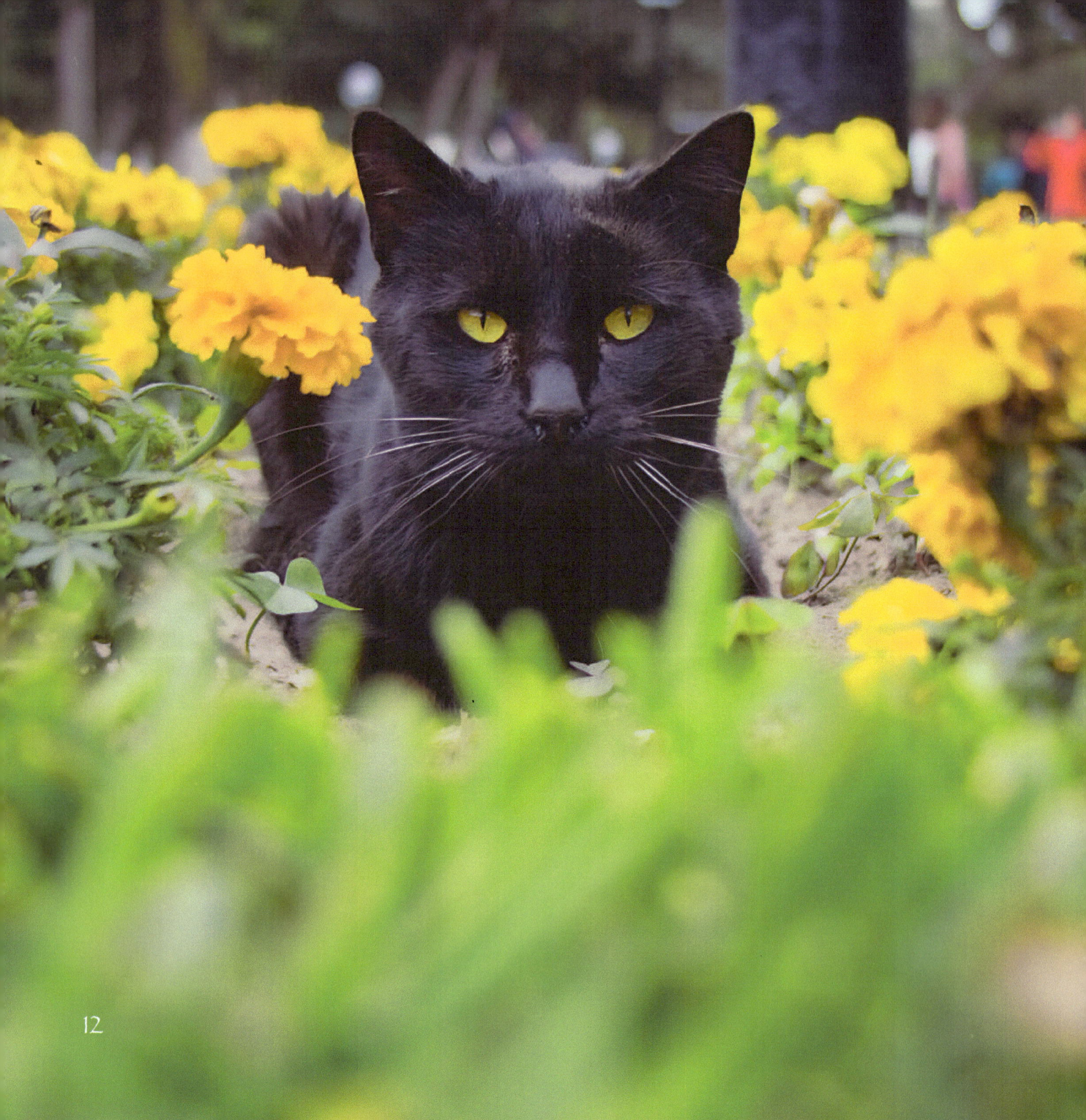

Lima is the fourth largest city in South America

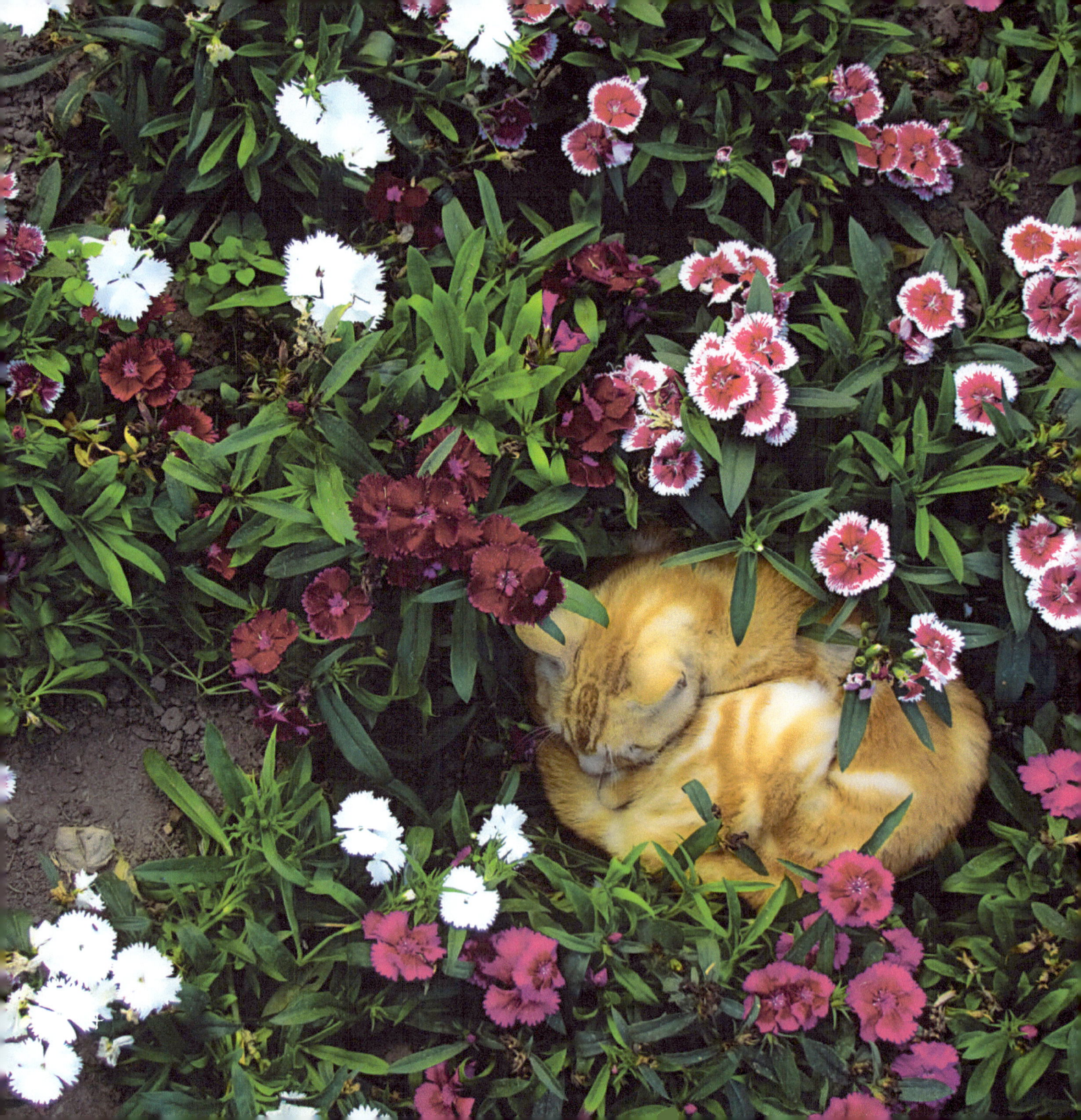

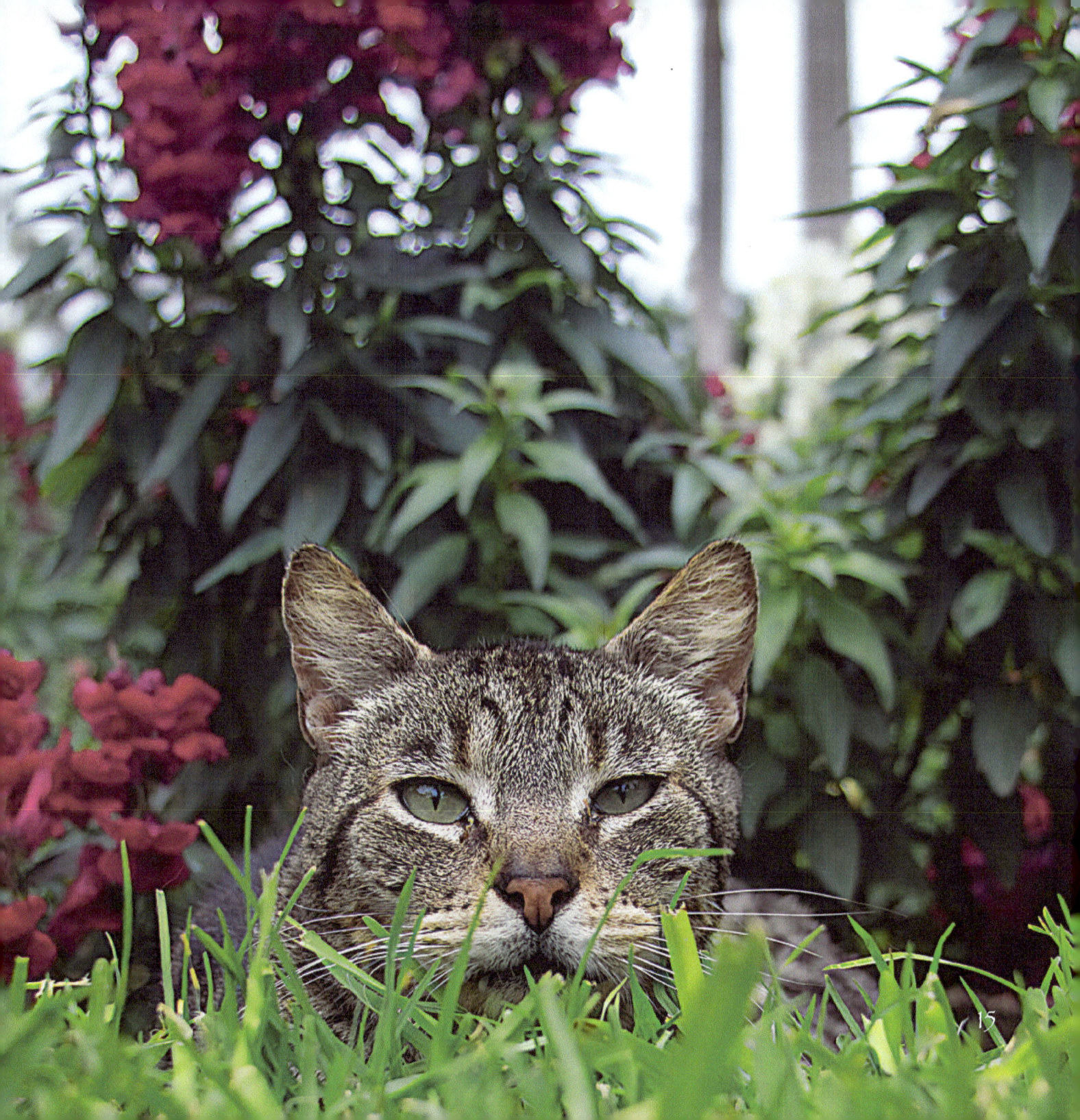

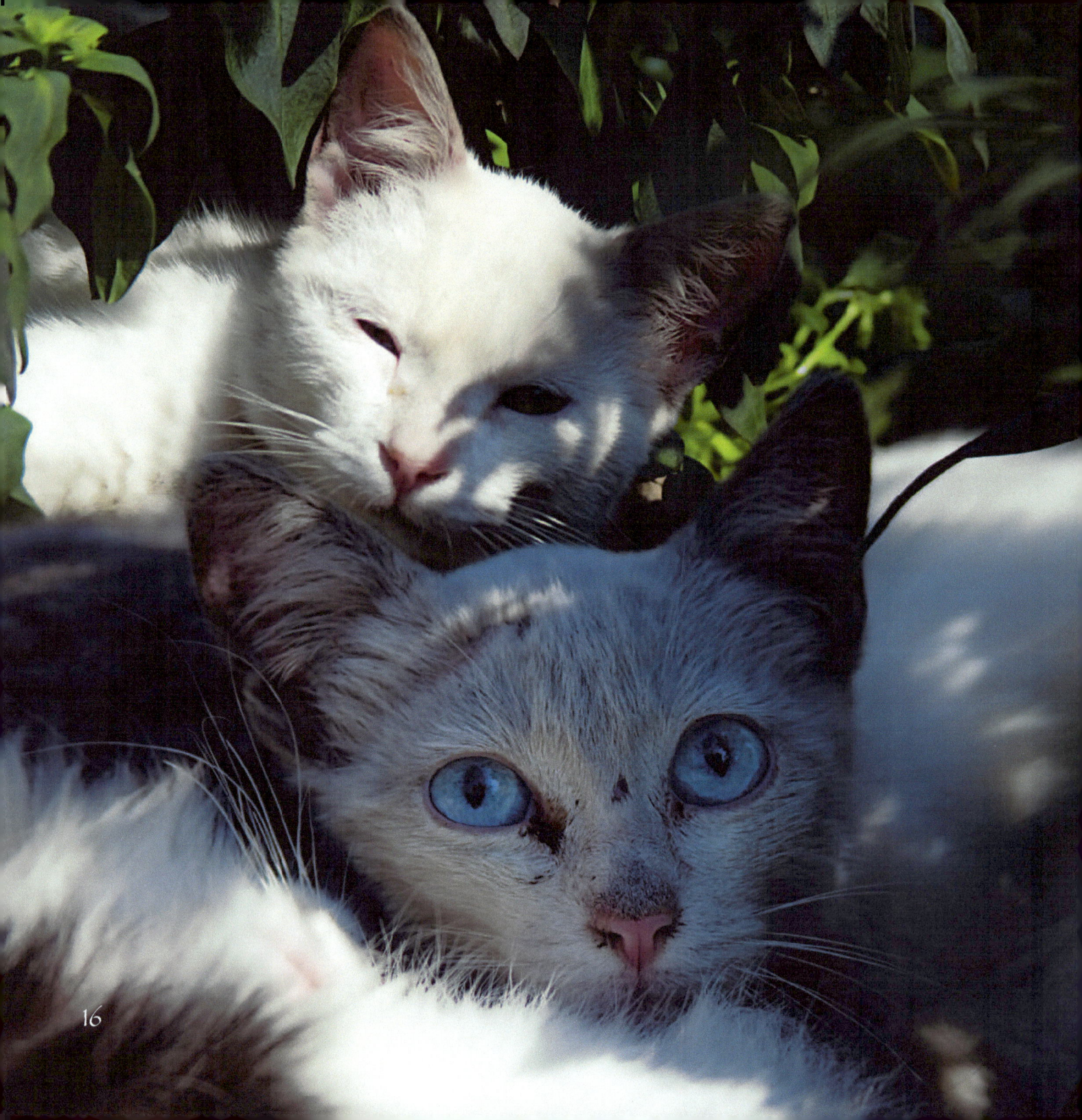

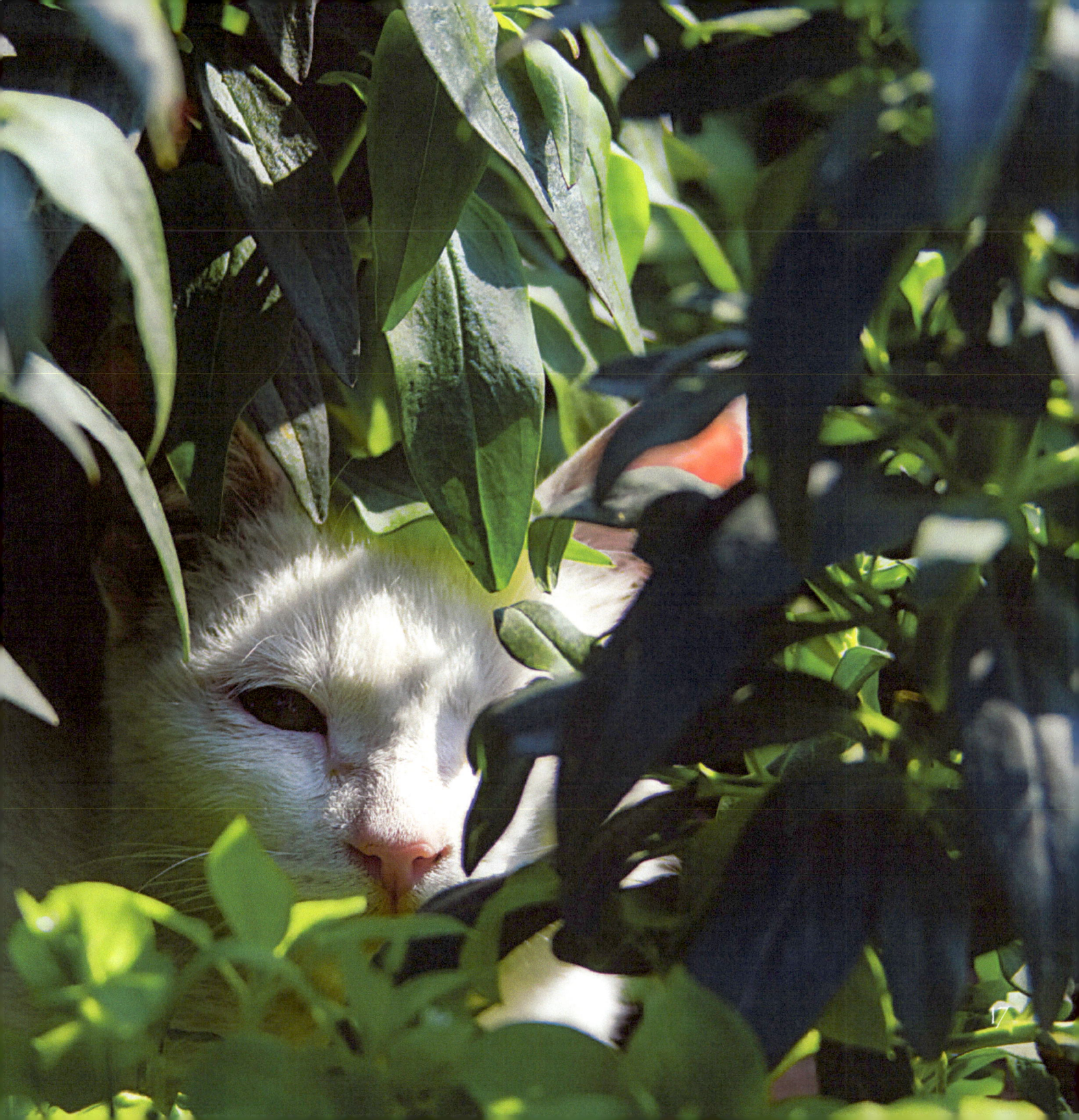

Today there are about 100 distinct breeds of the domestic cat

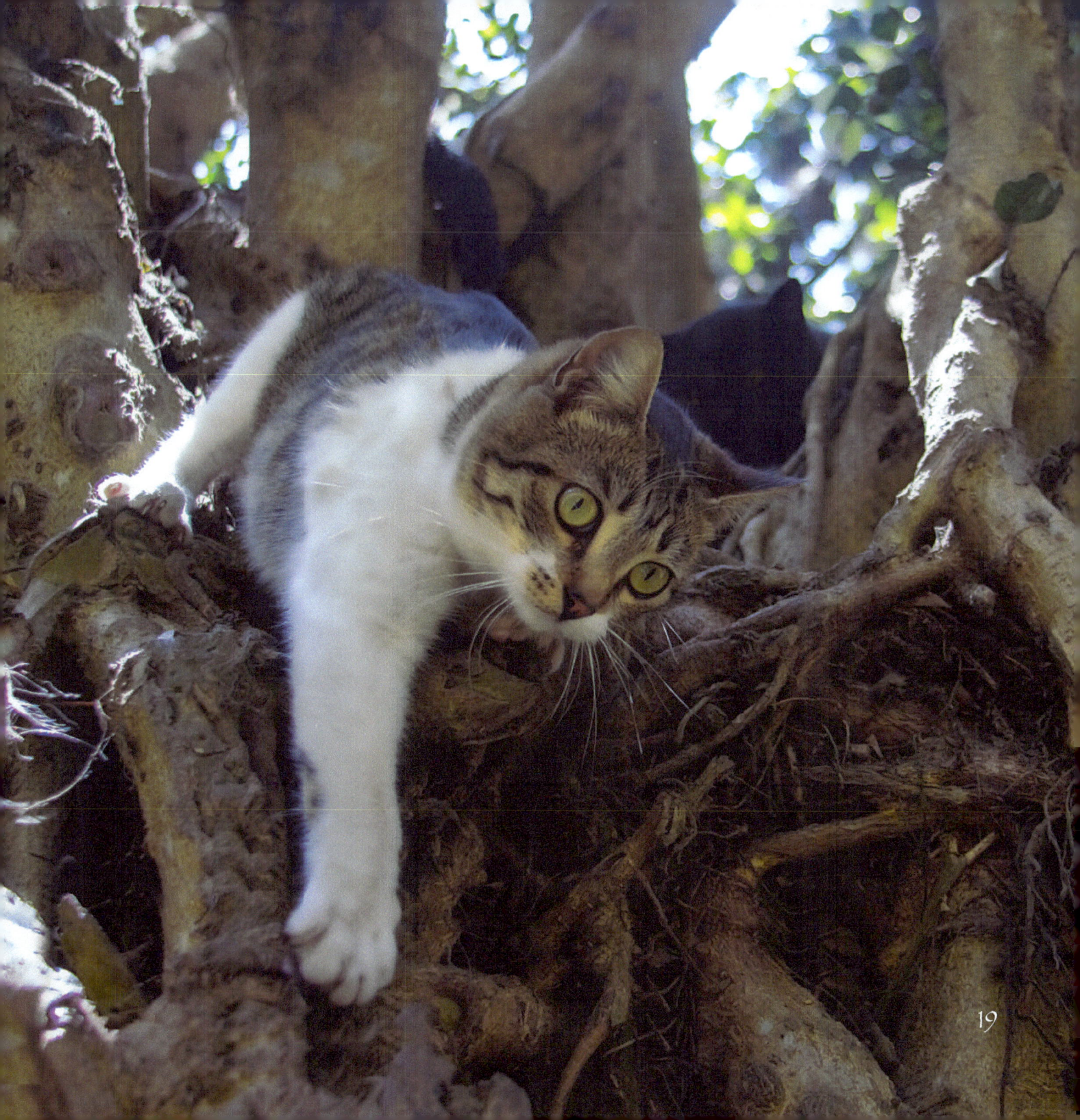

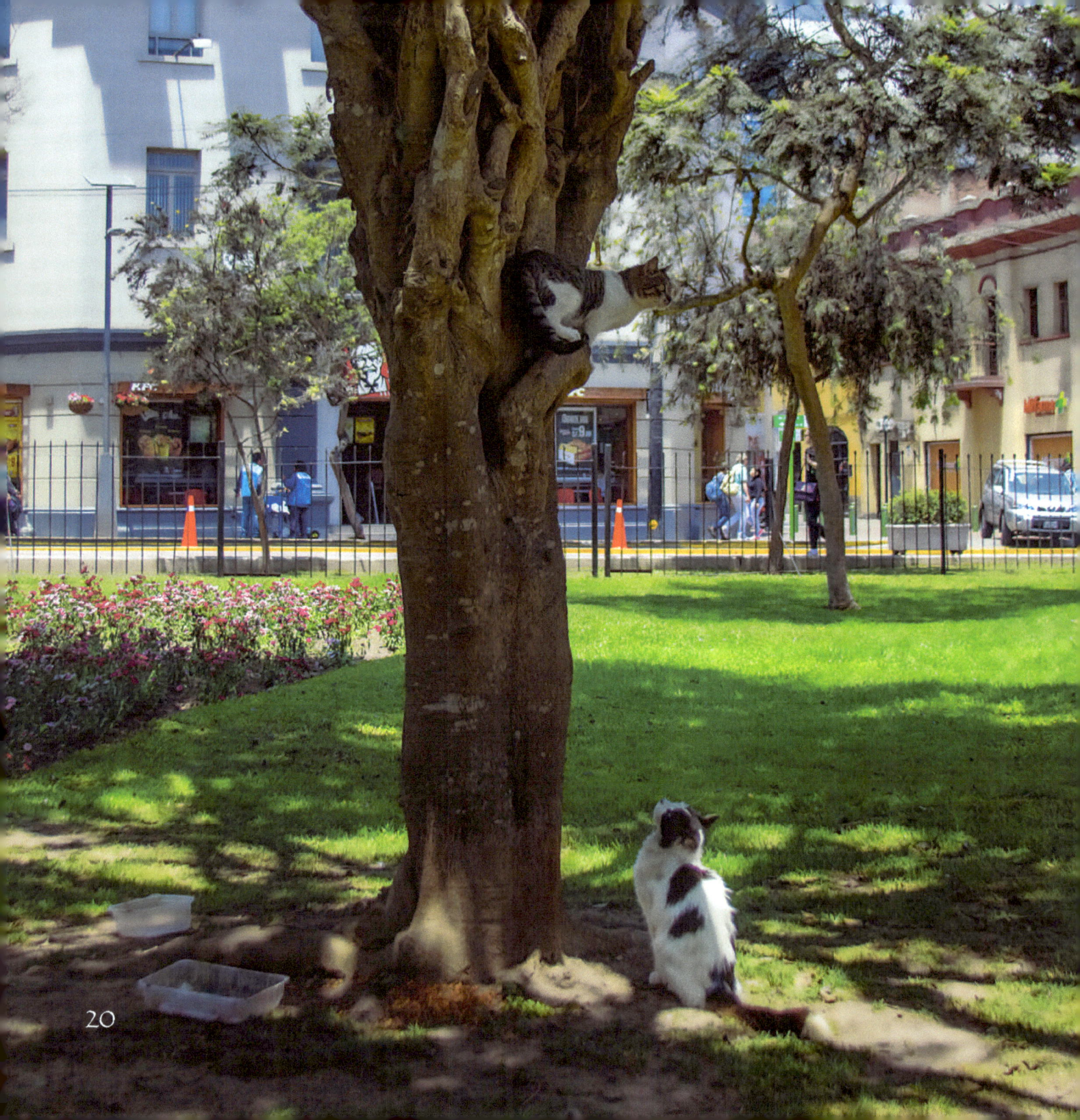

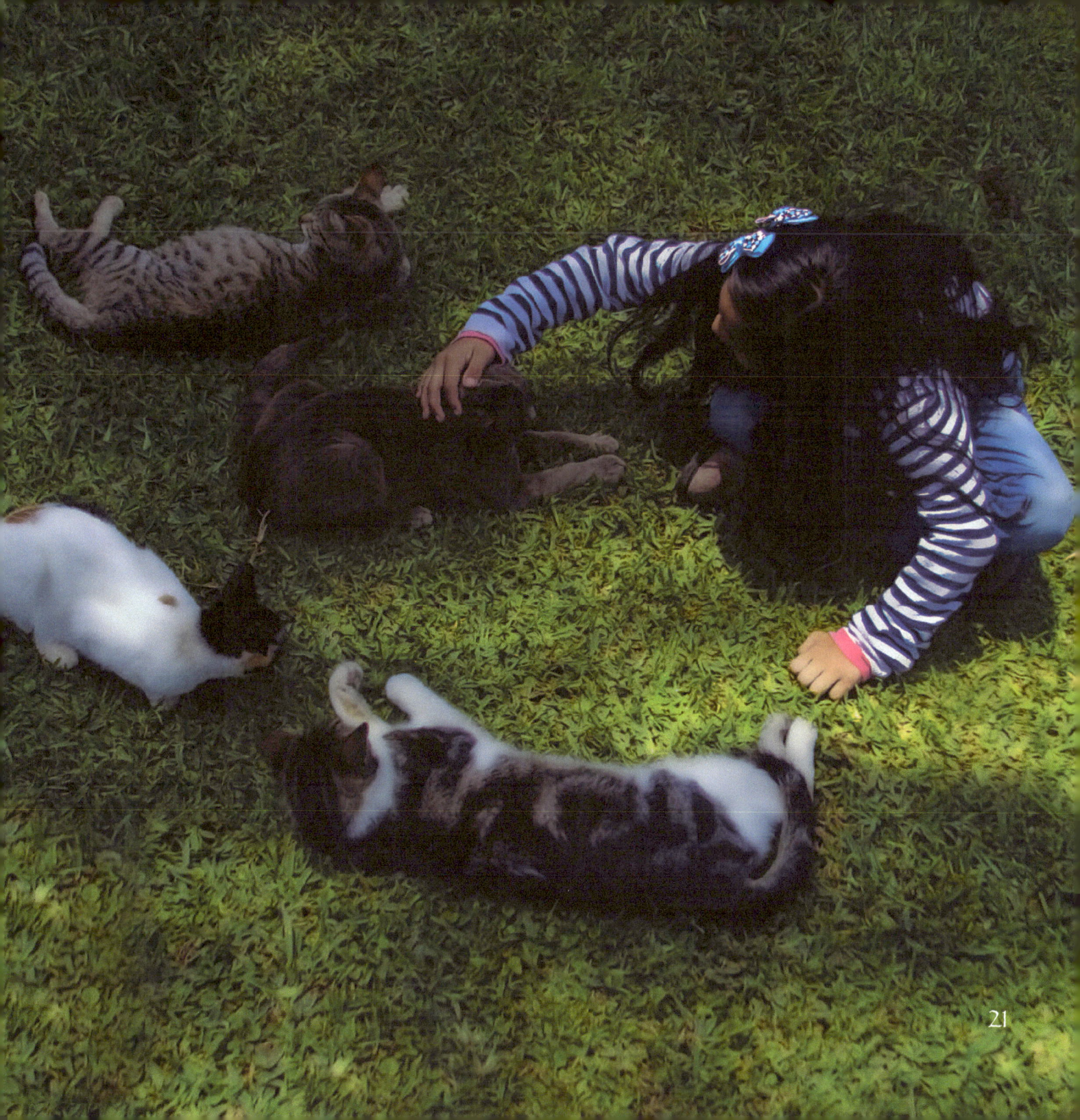

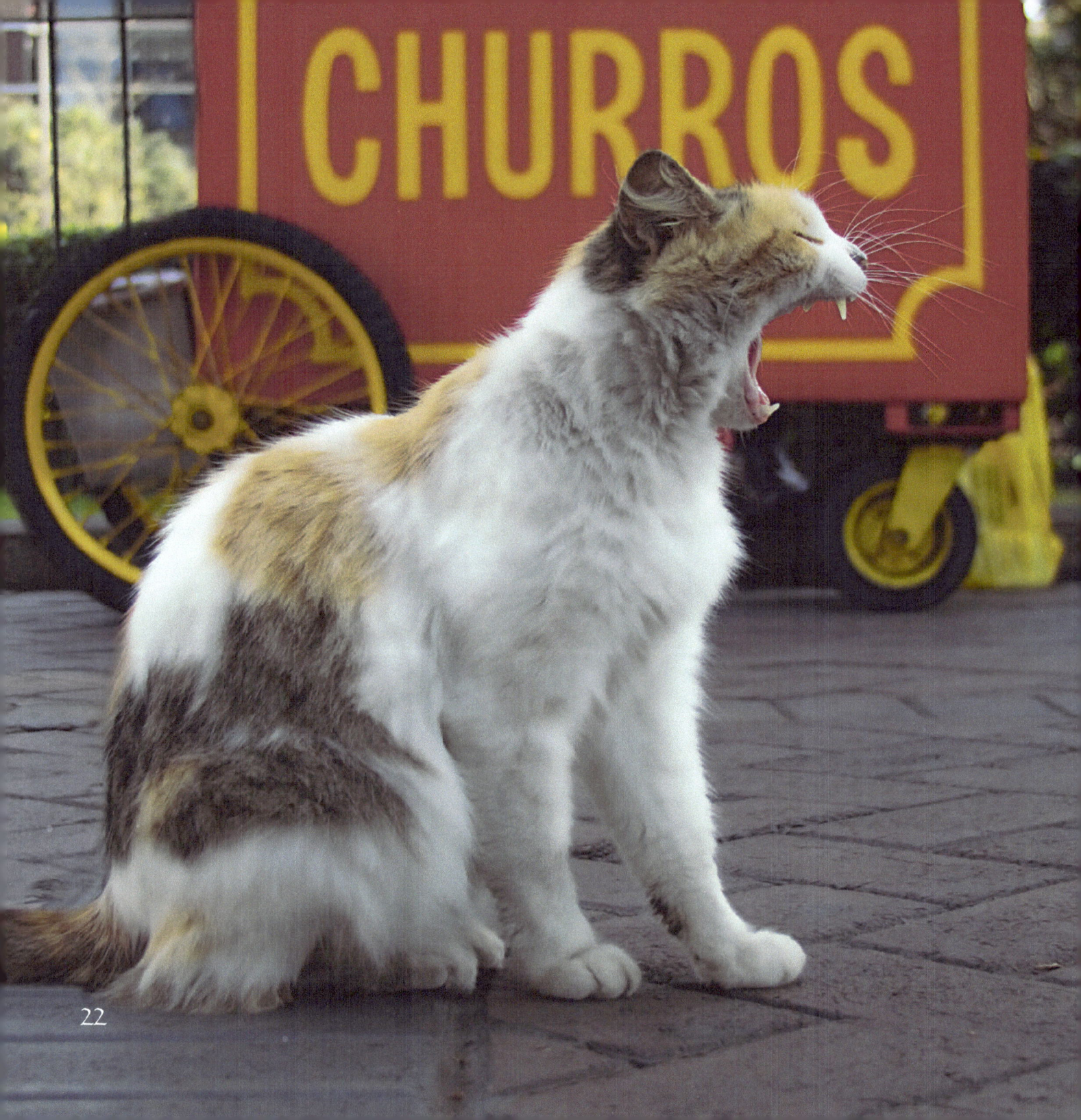

Lima is located on a strip of desert between the
Pacific Ocean and Andes Mountain

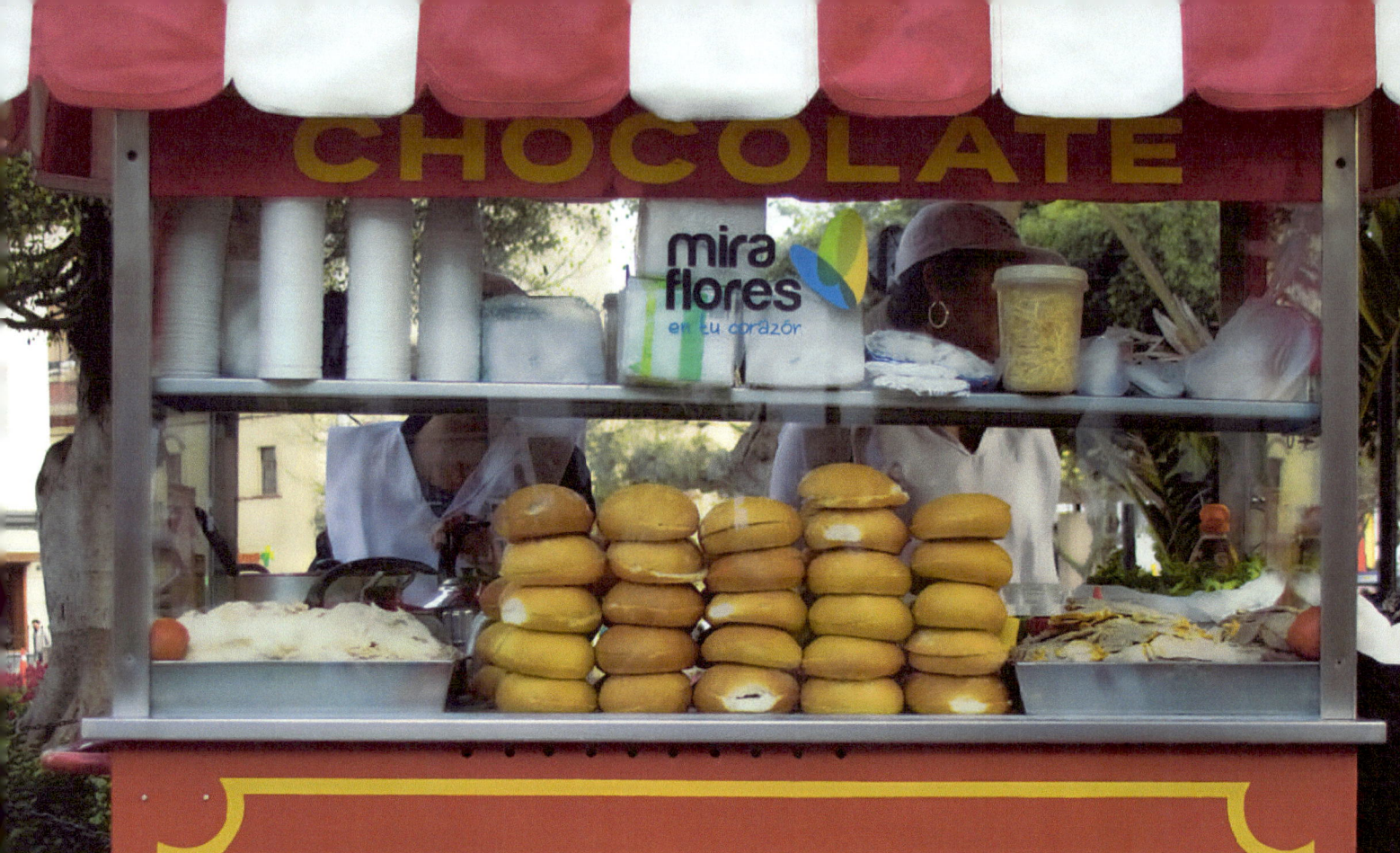

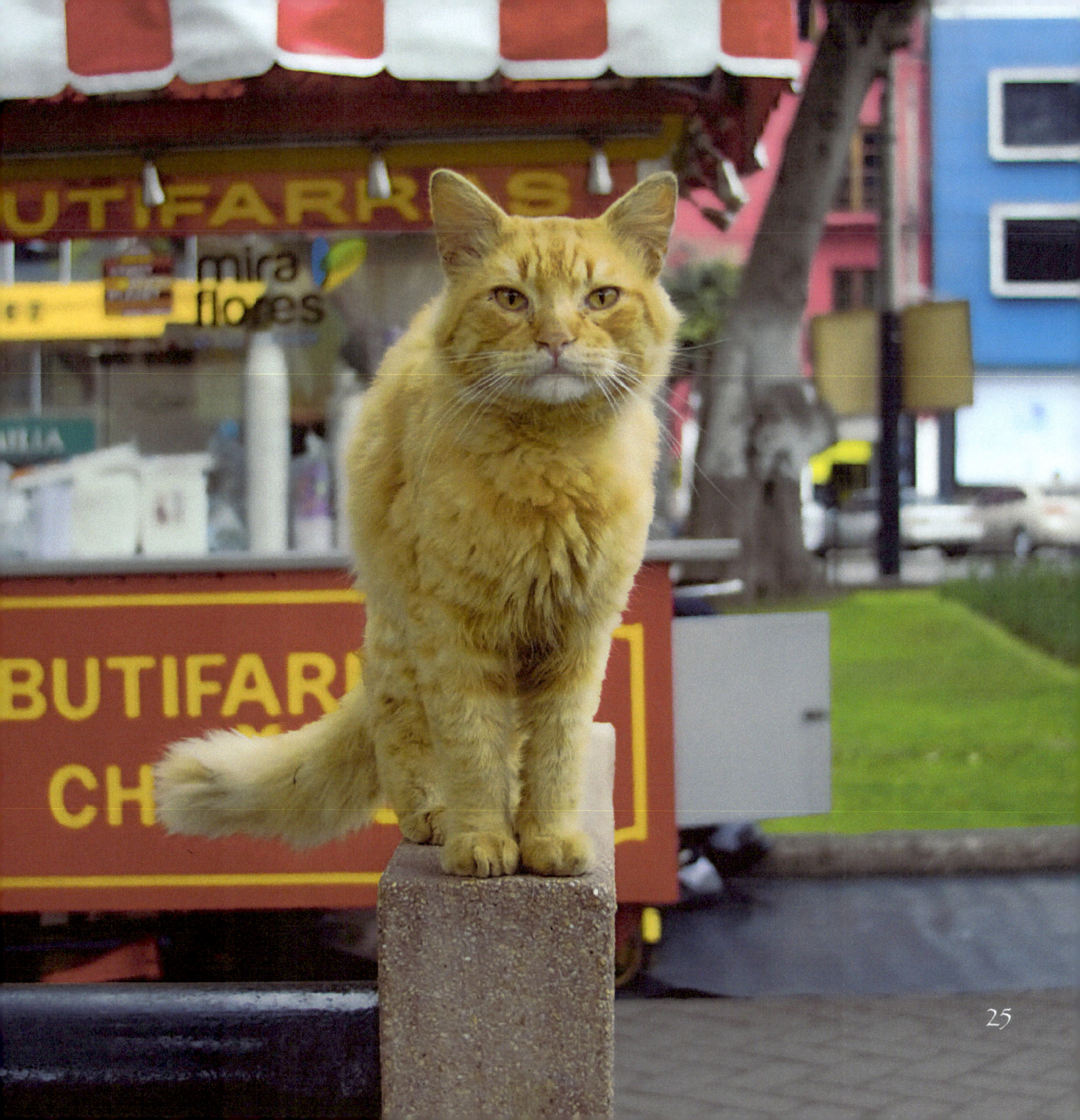

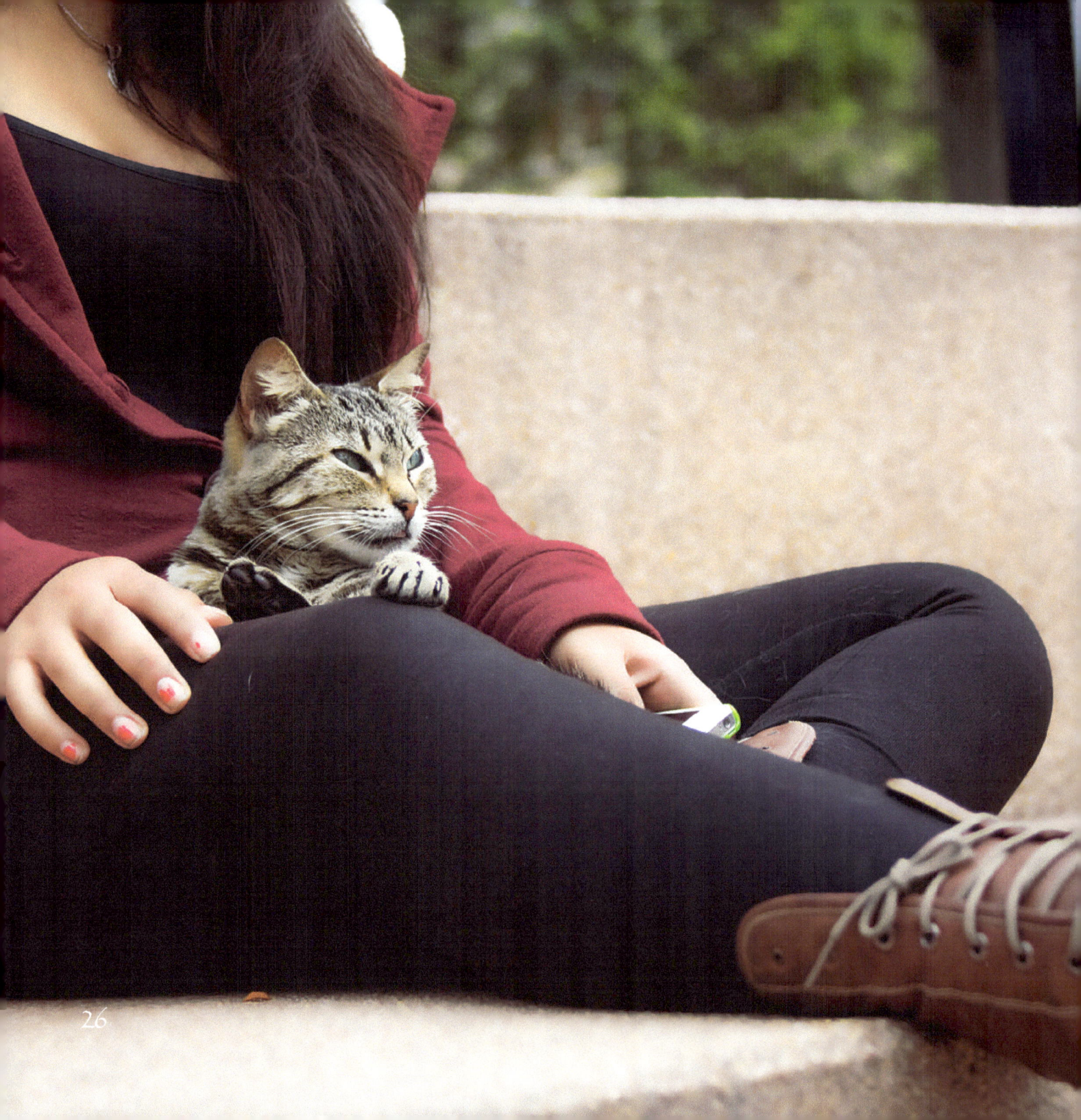

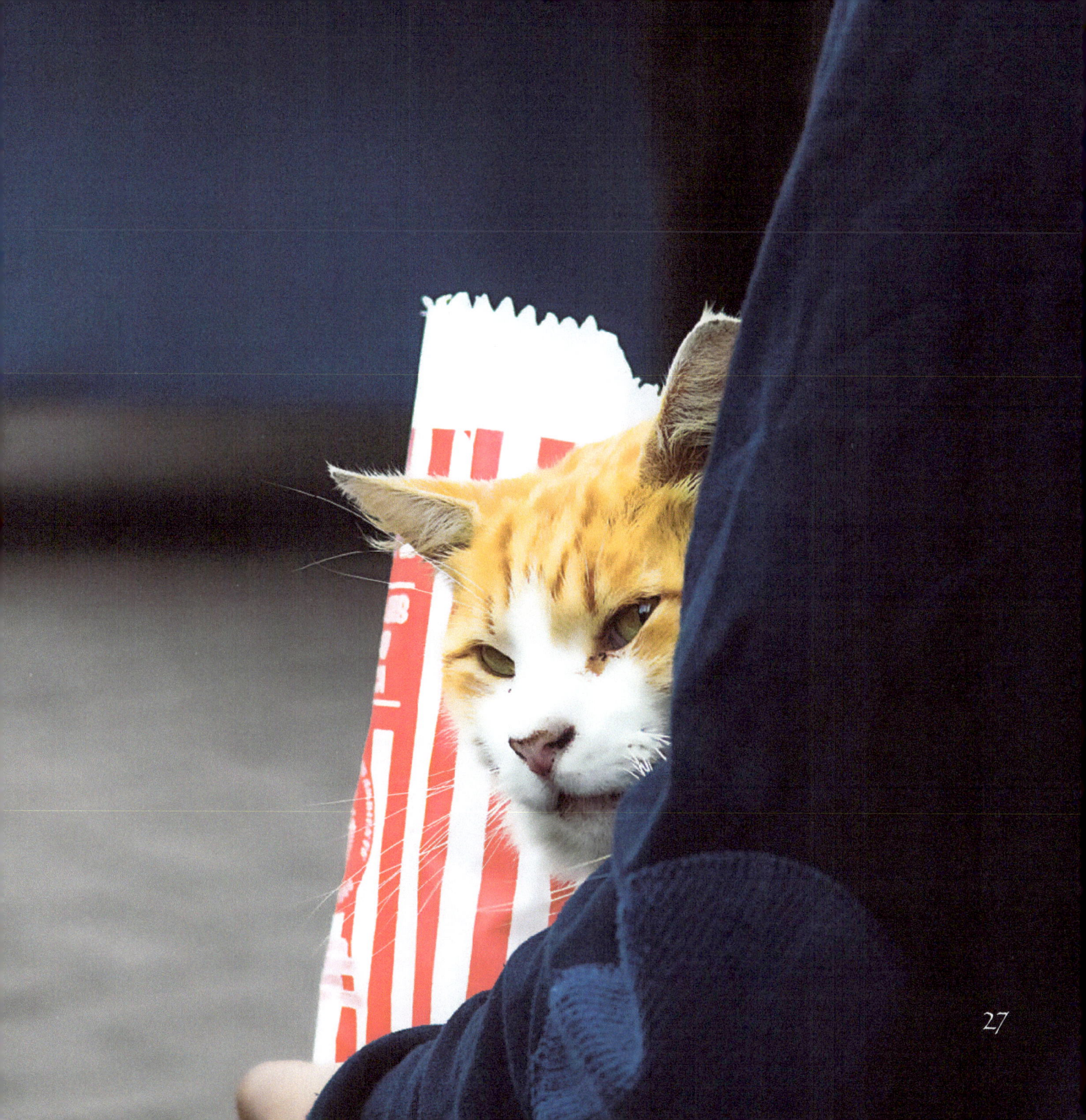

The catnip plant contains oil called nepetalactone, which affects cats like marijuana affects humans

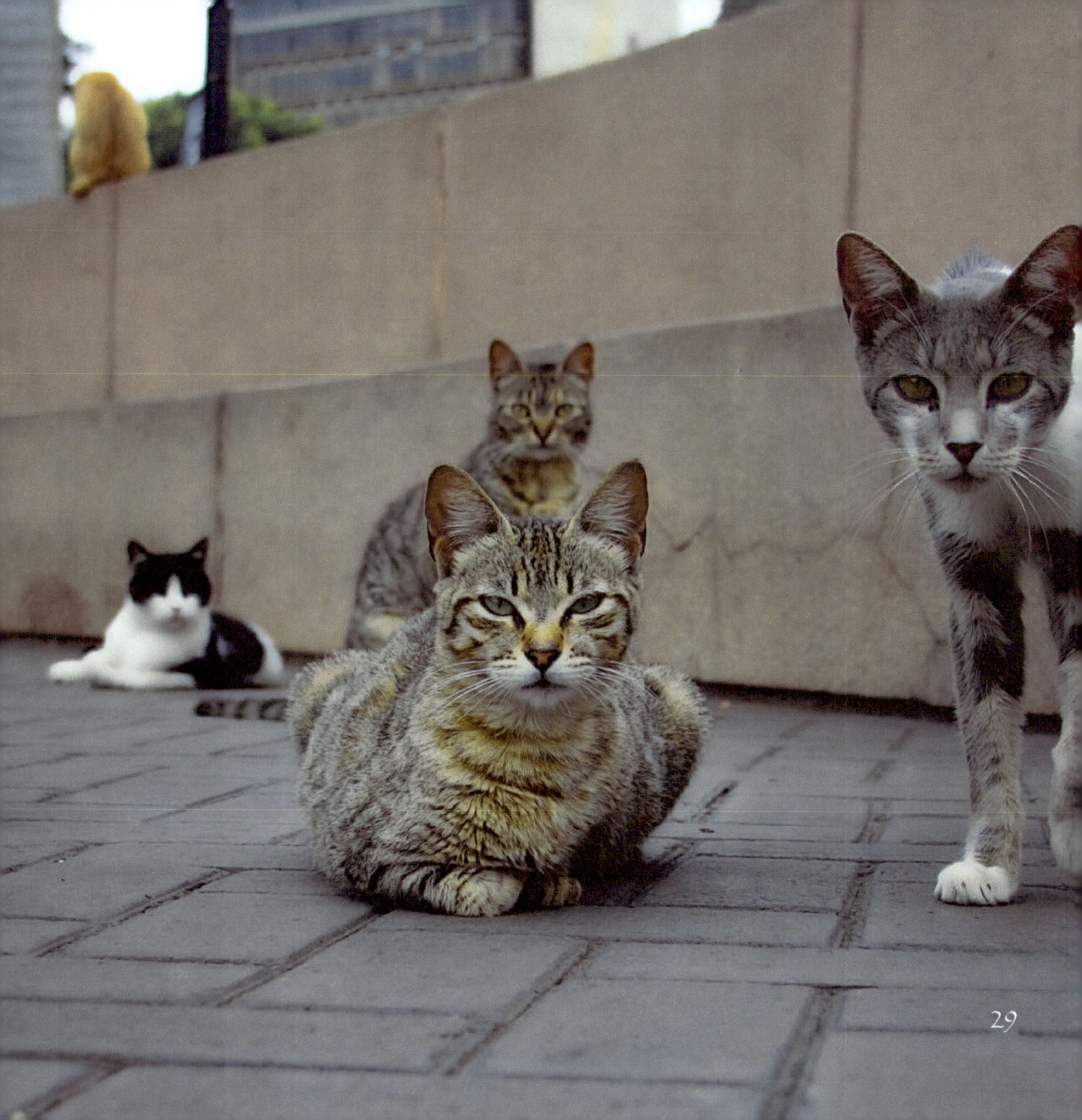

29

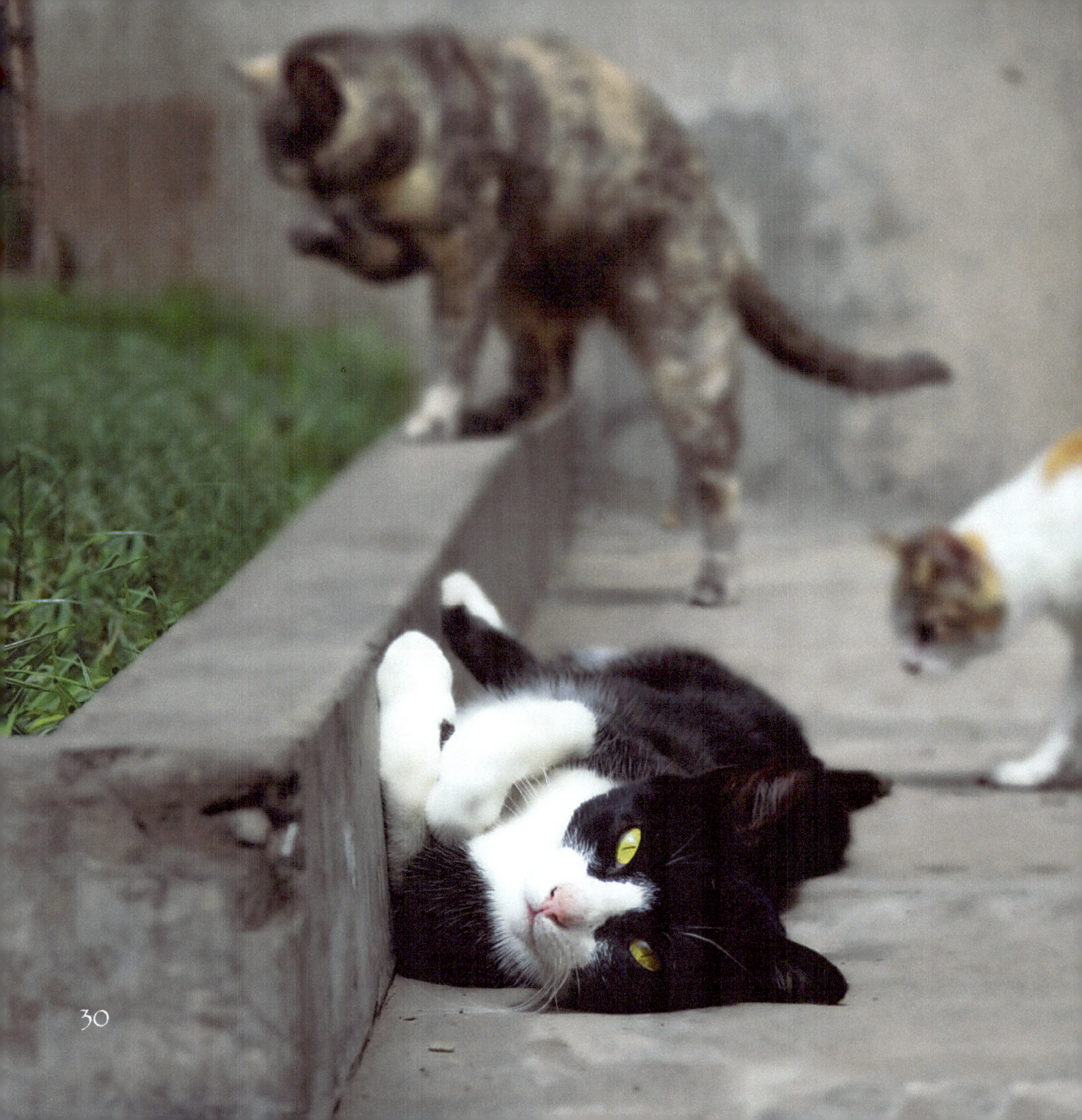

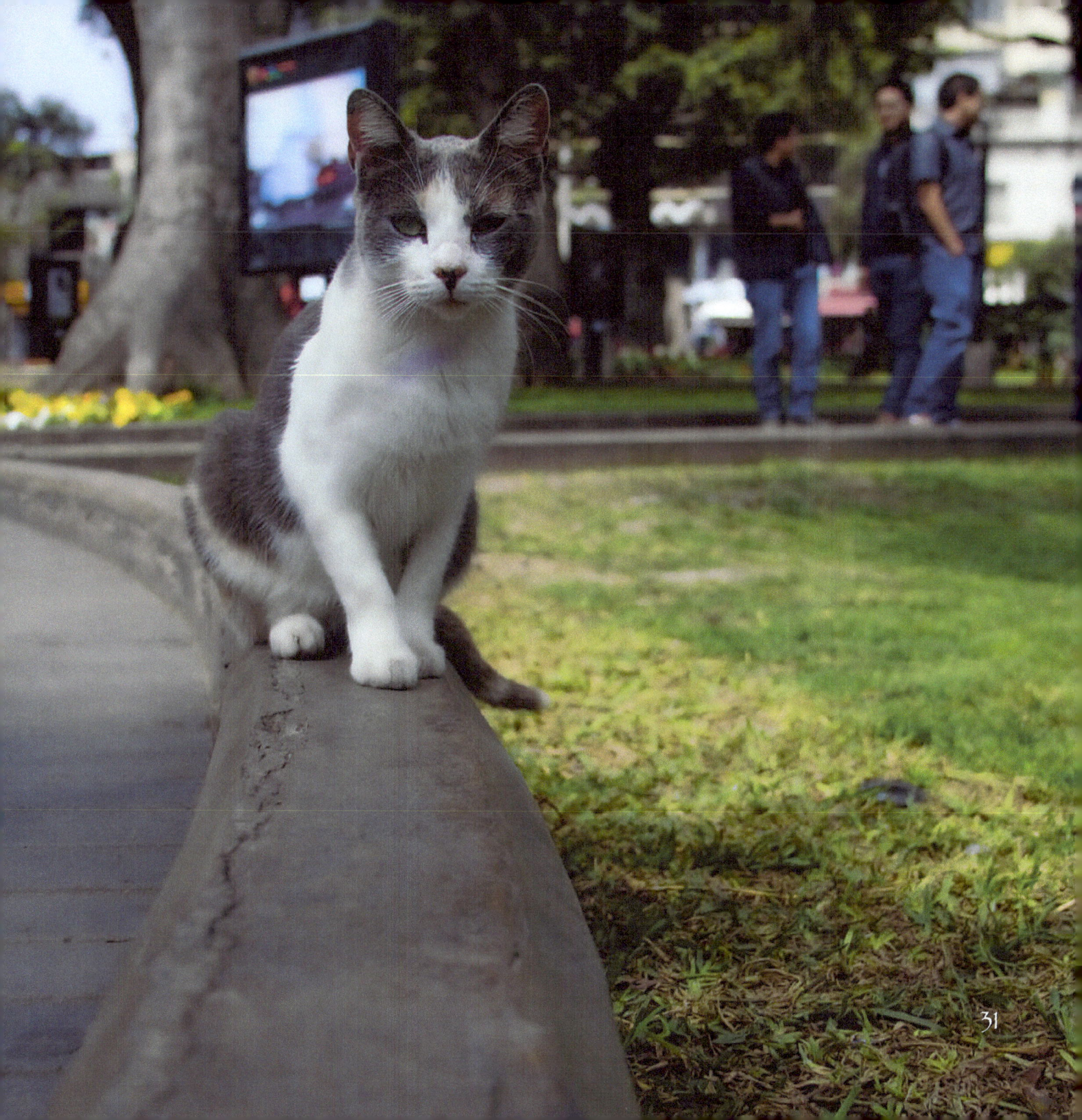

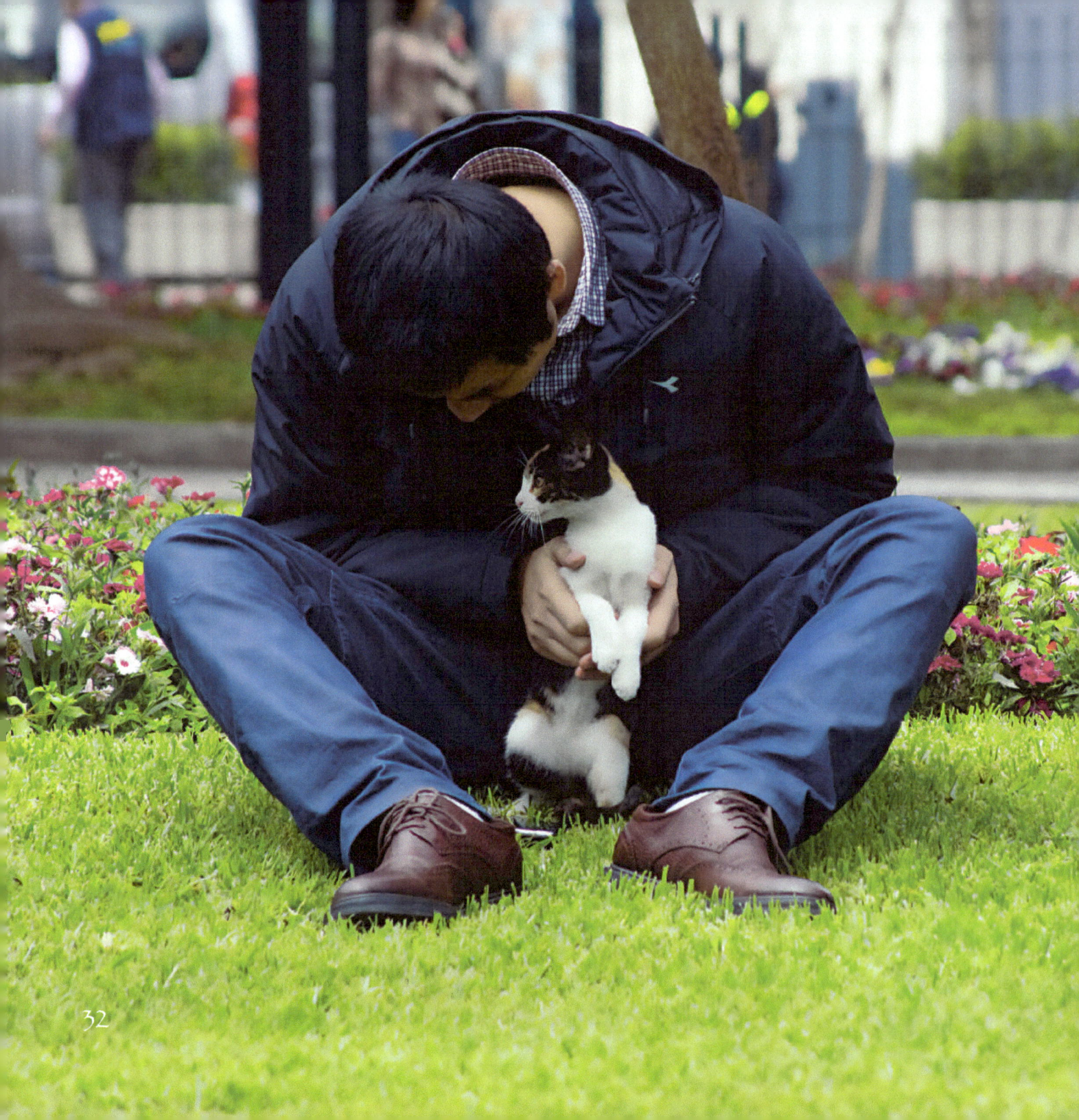

Residents of Lima are known as Limeños

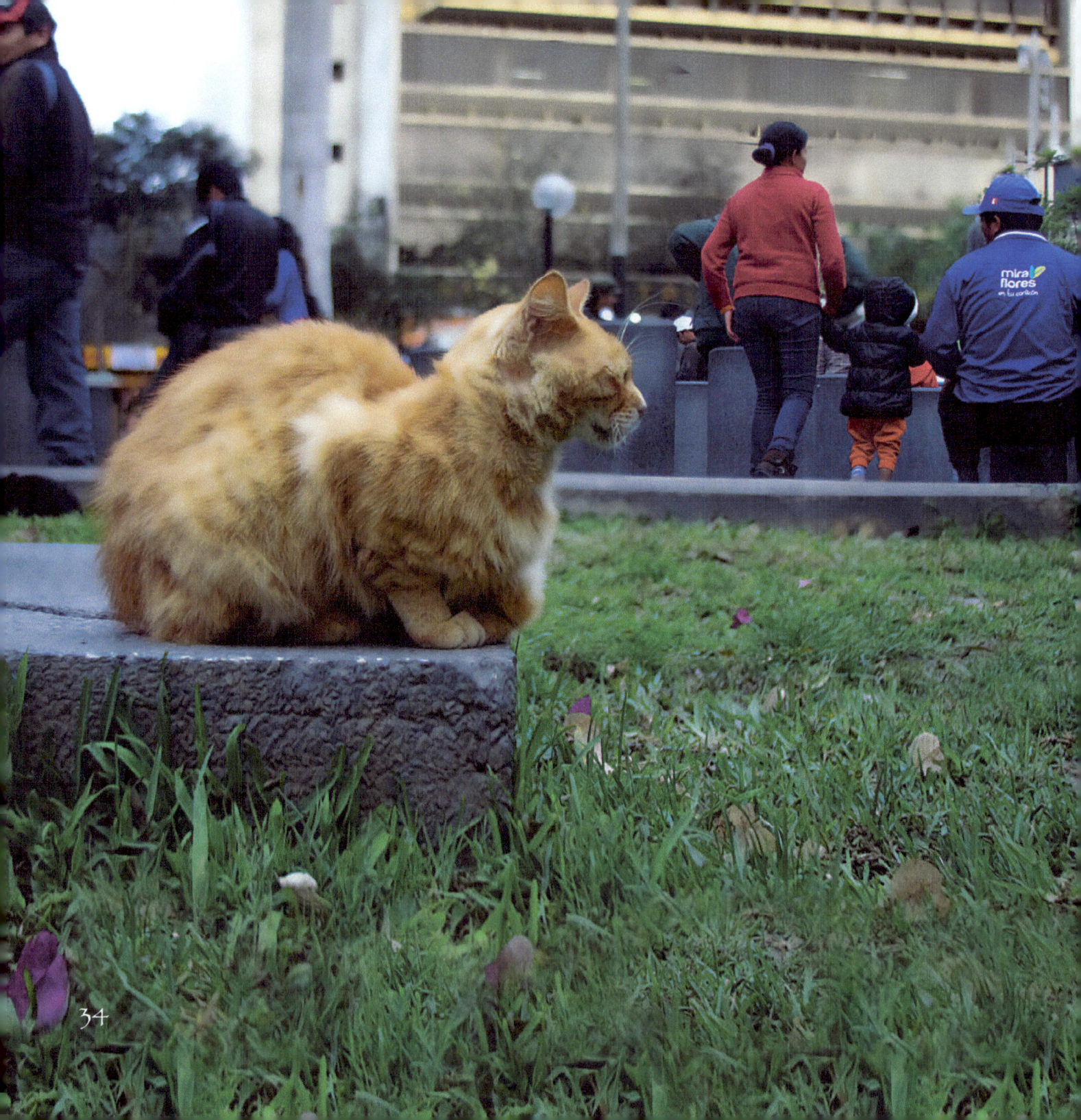

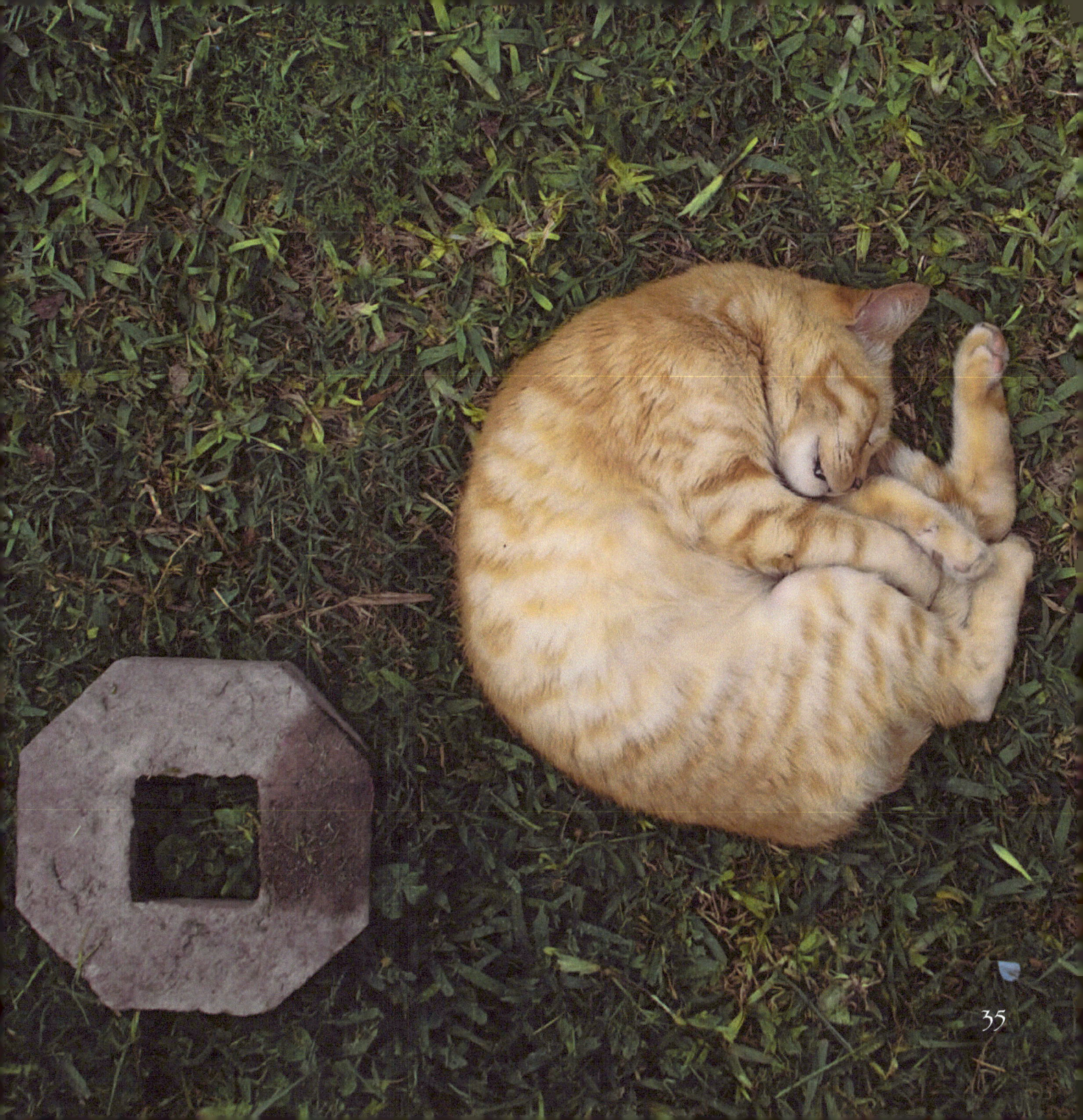

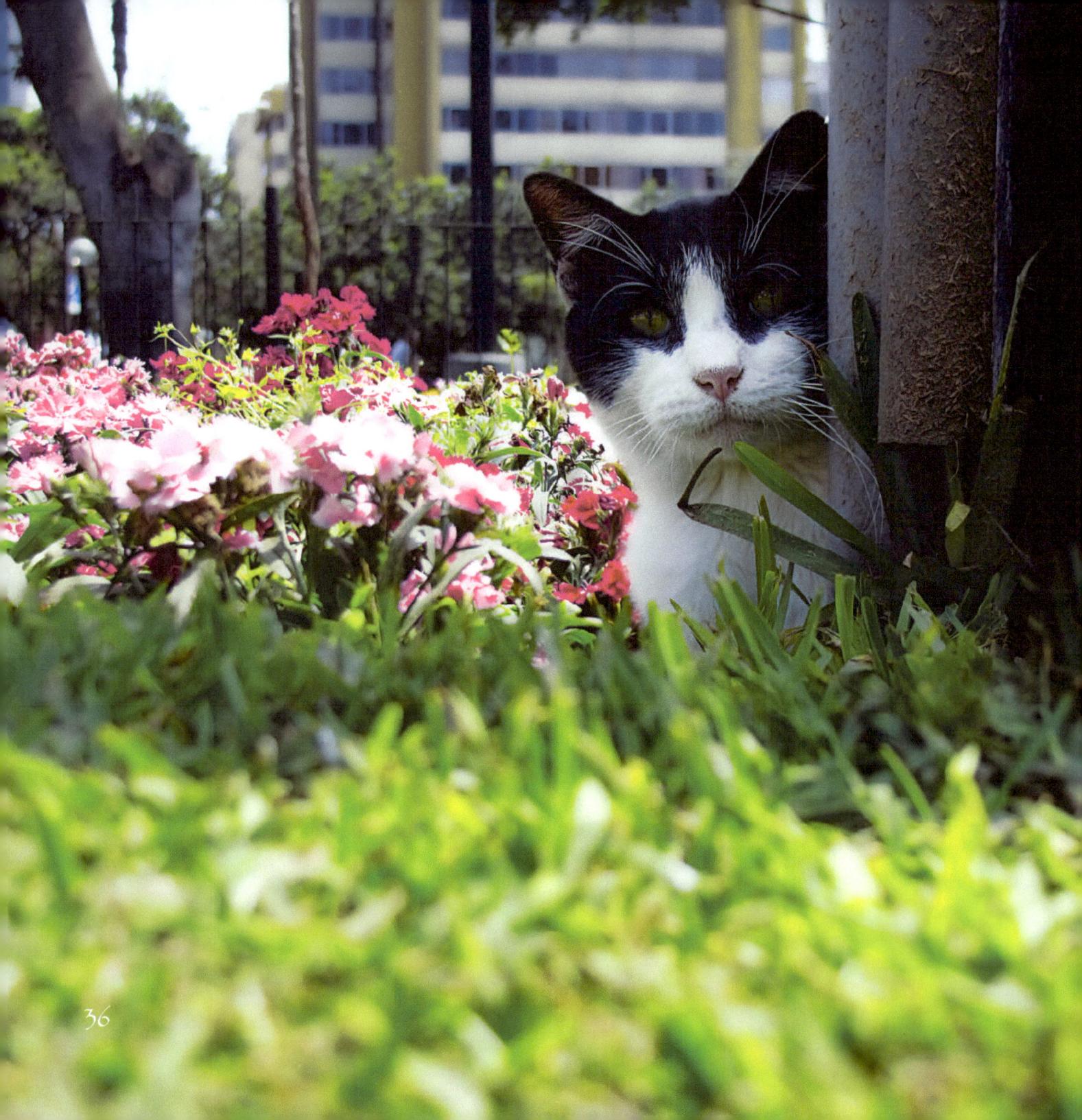

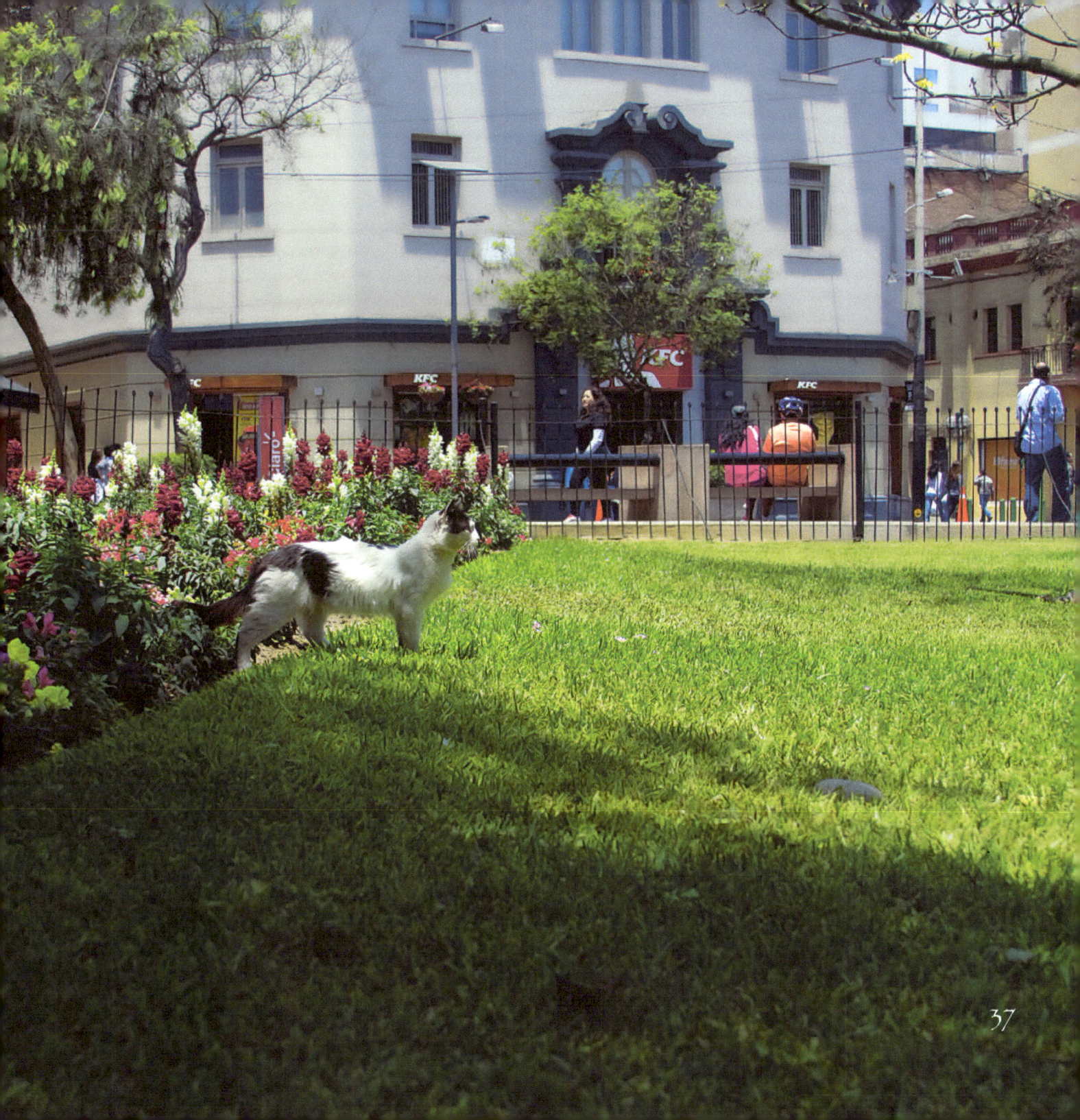

The smallest domestic breed of cat is the Singapuras

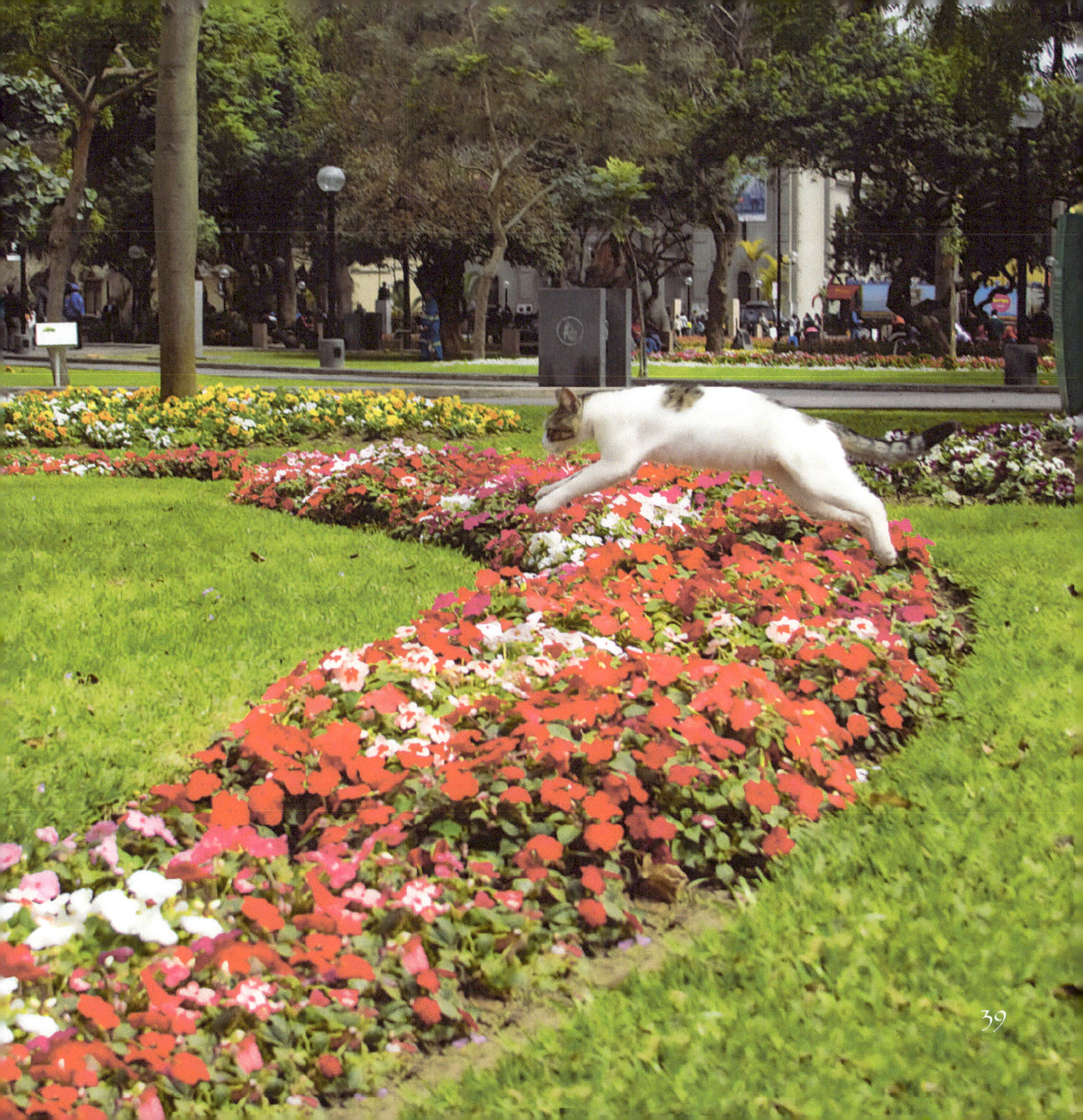

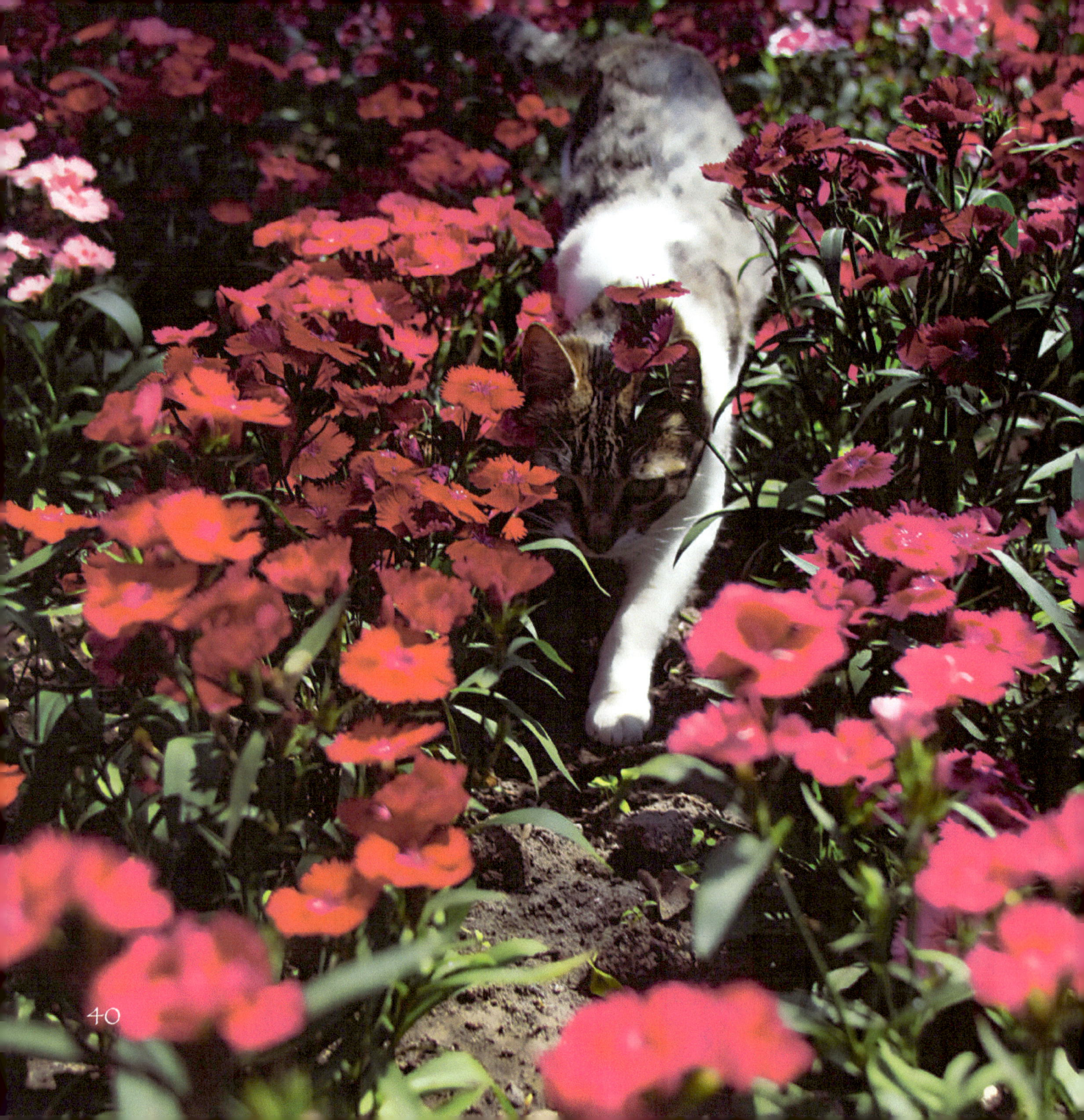

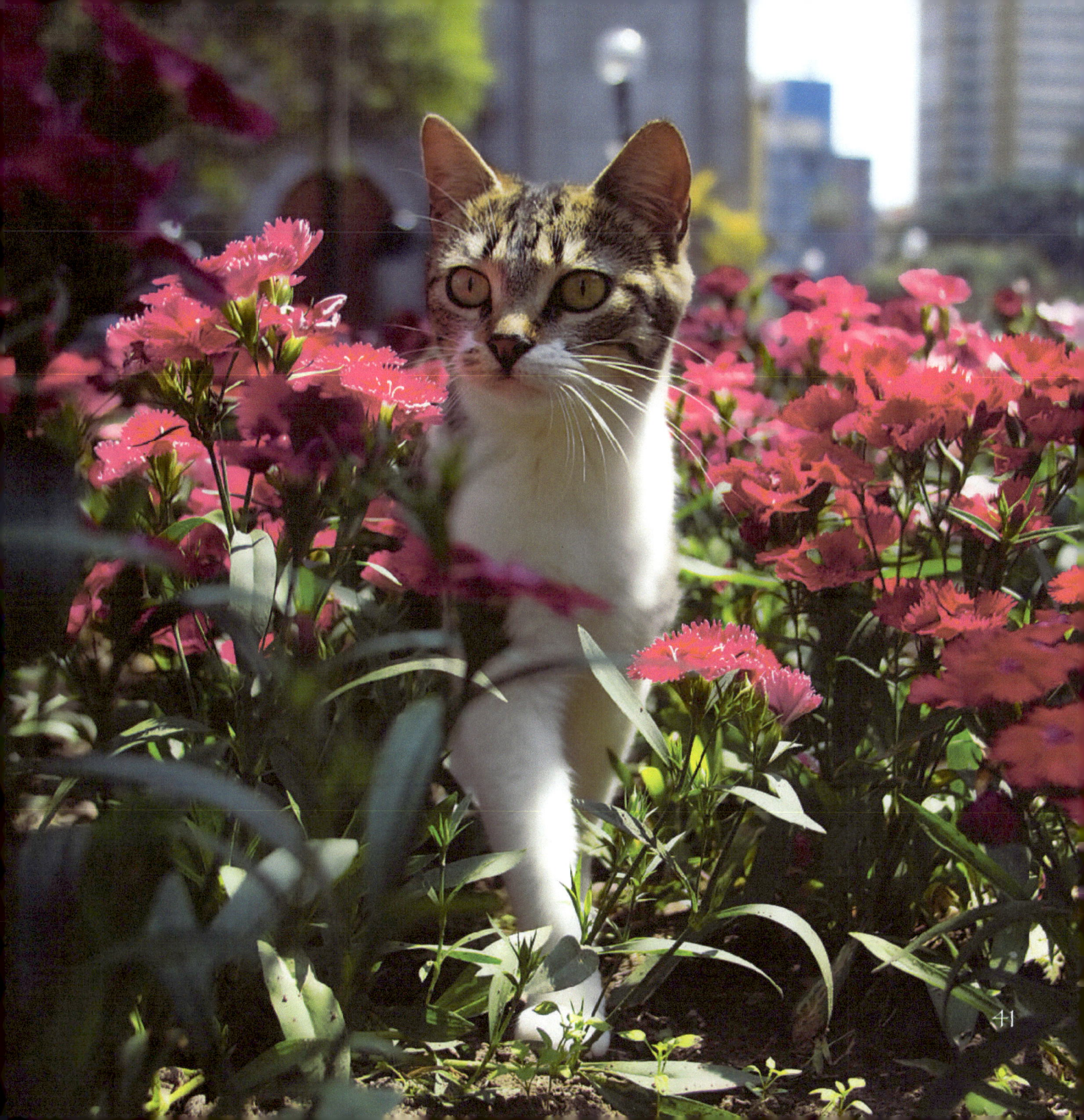

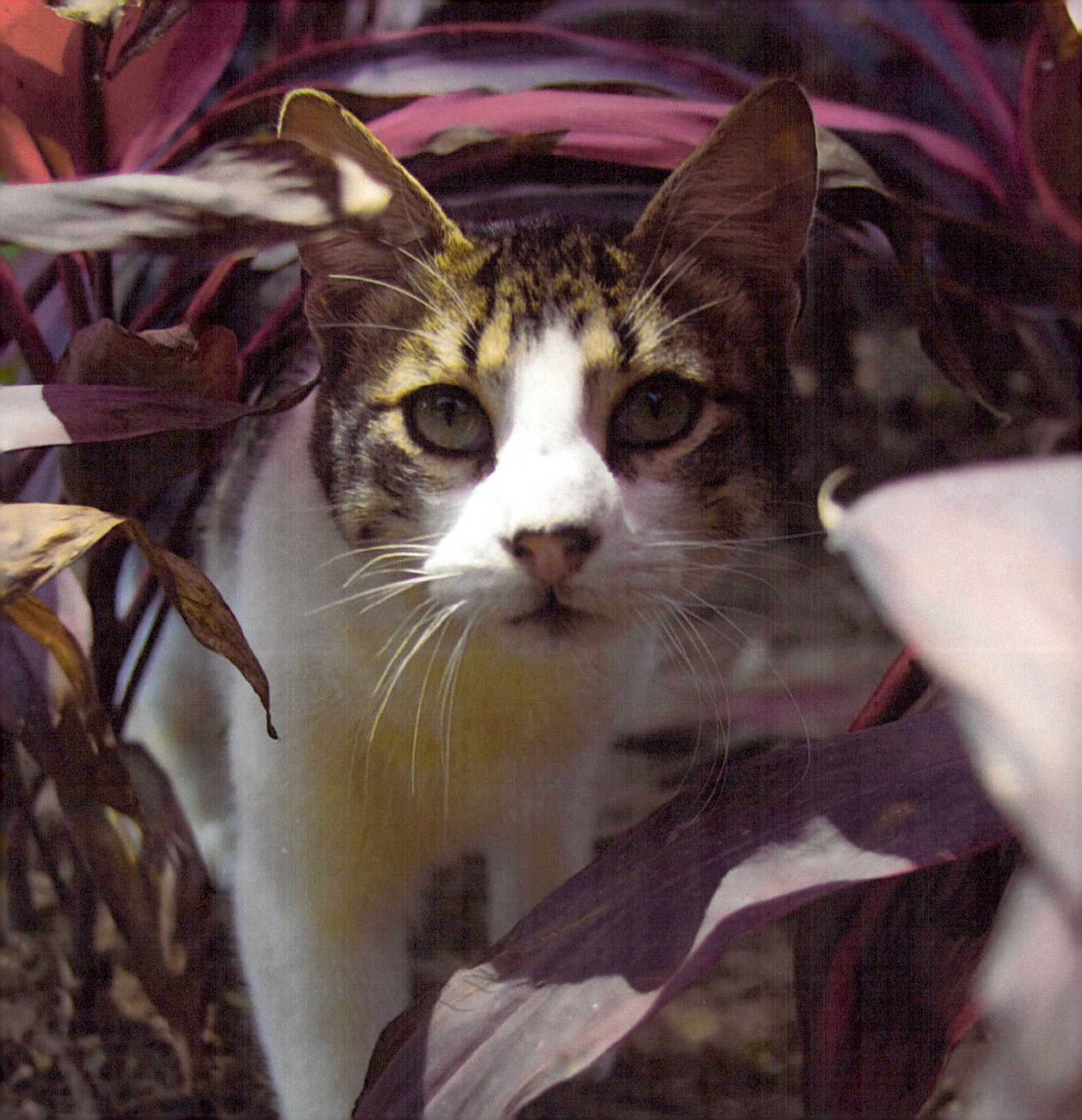

A third of Peru's population calls Lima home

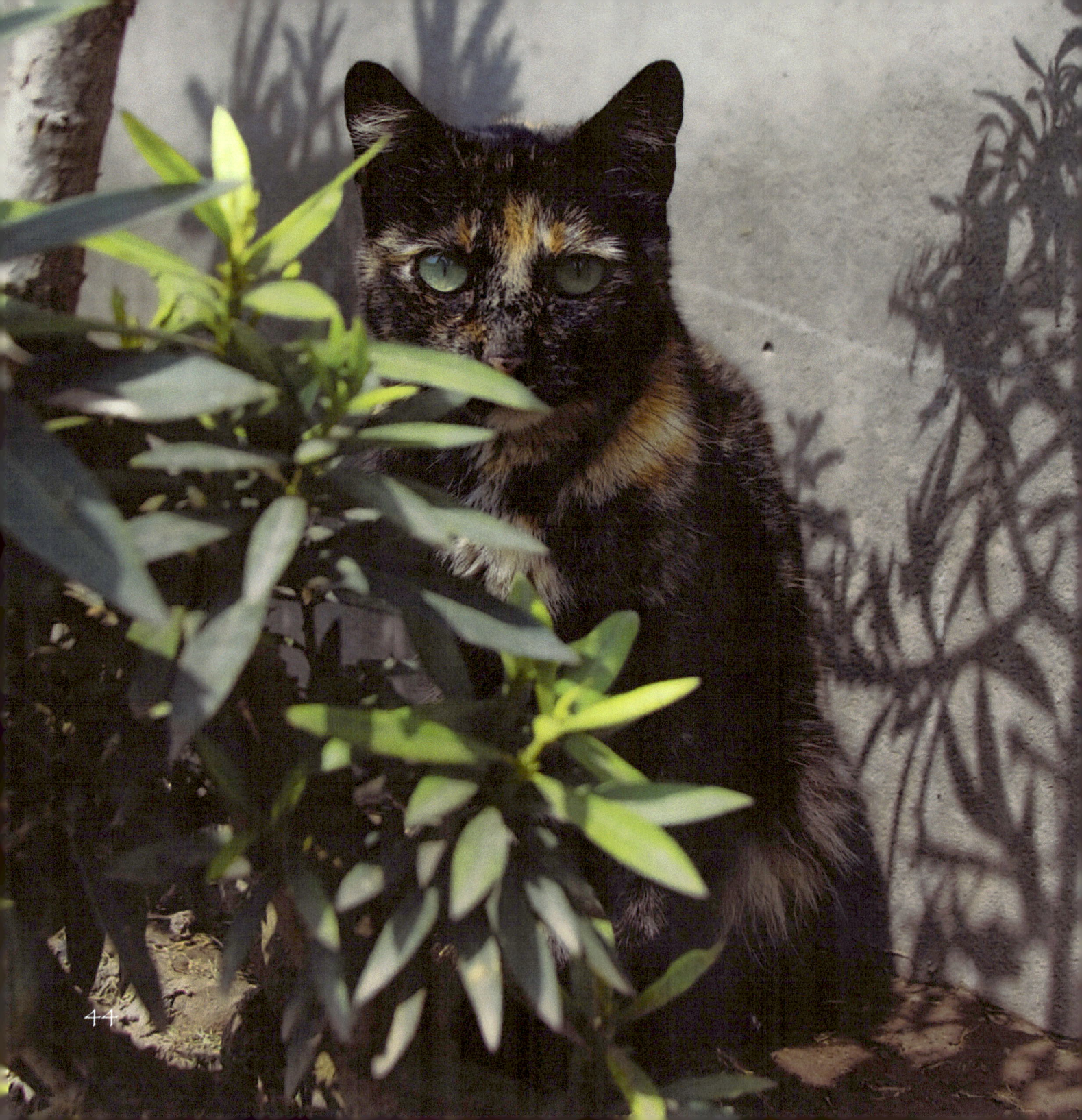

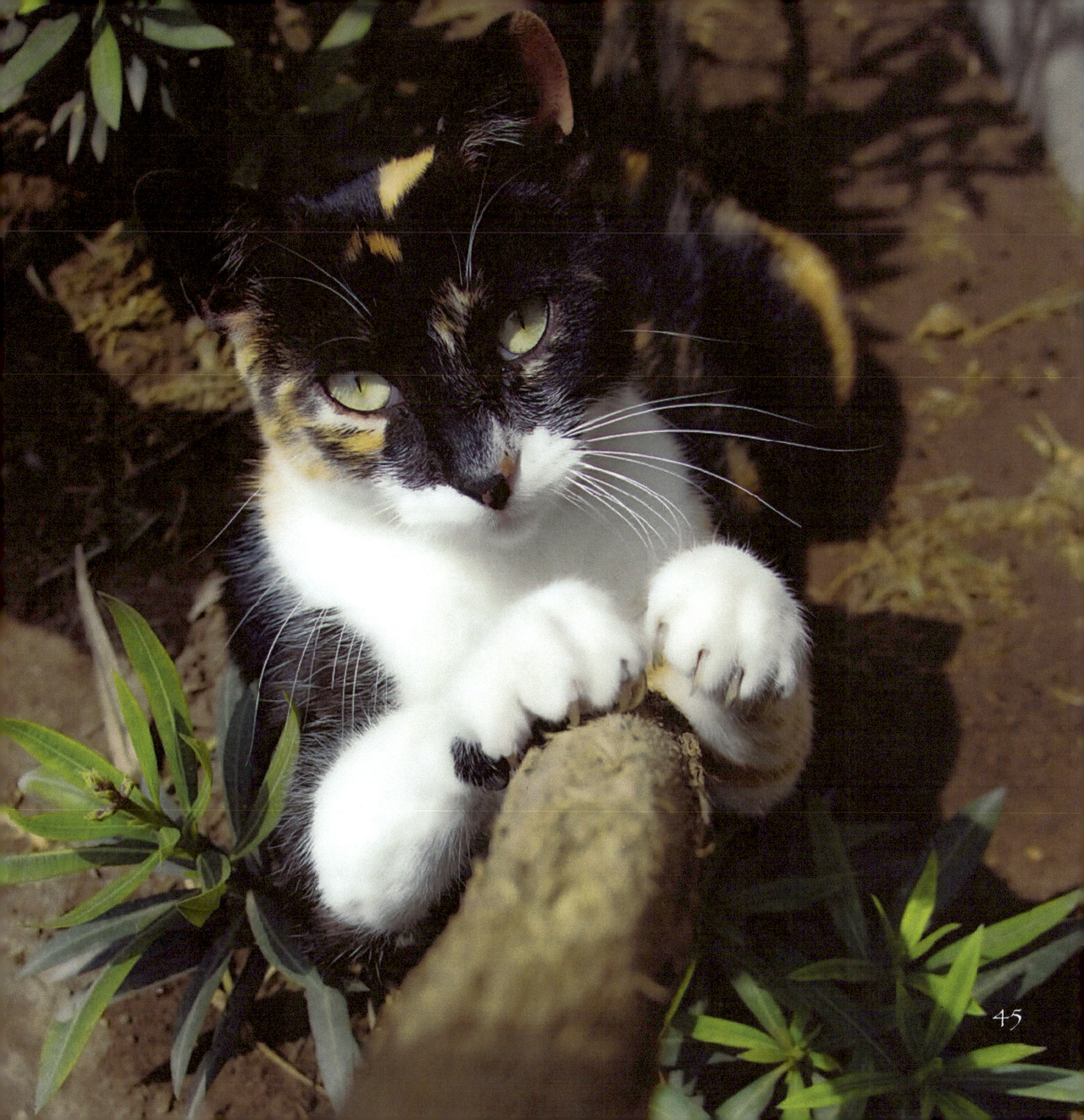

45

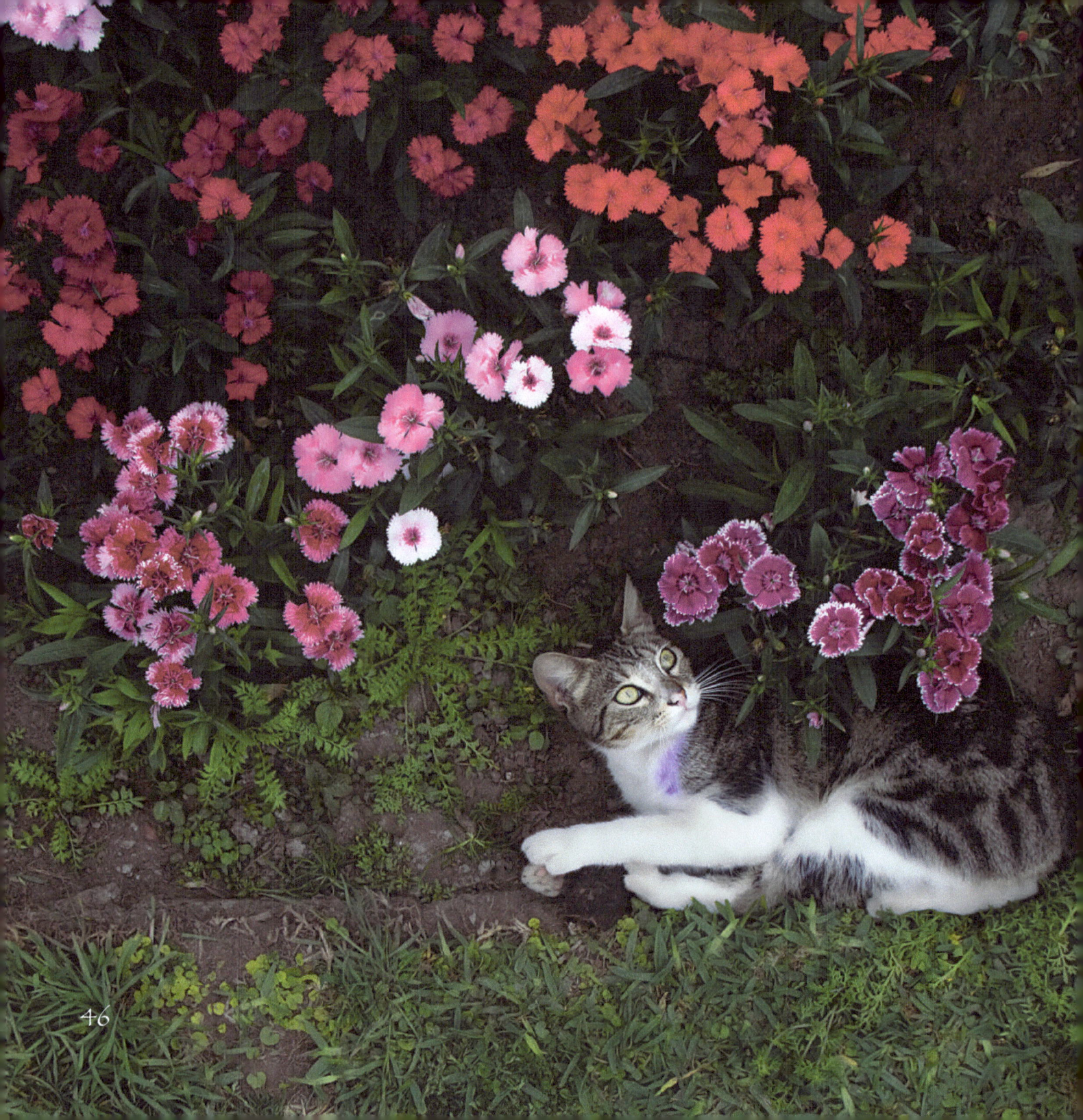

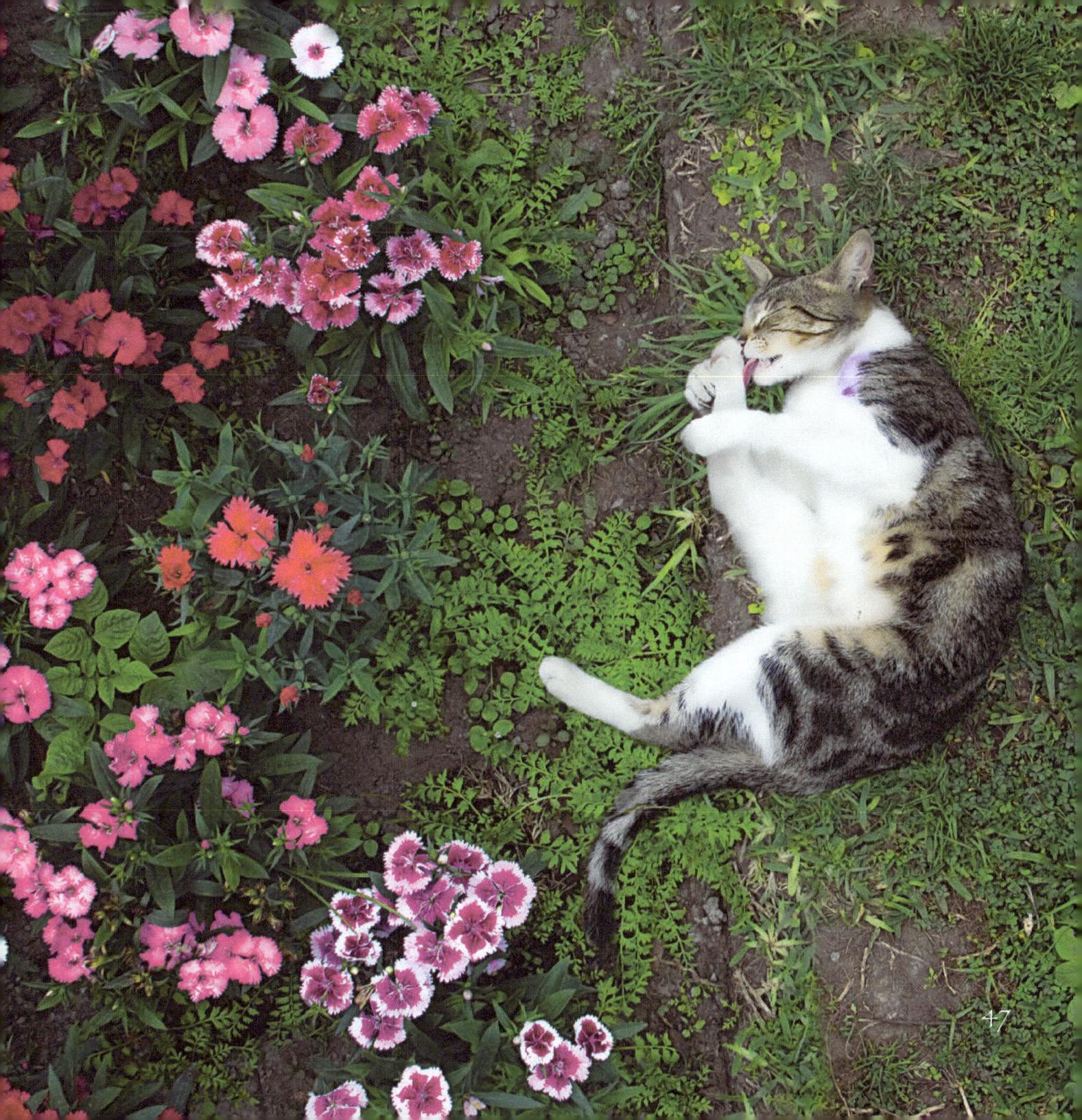

The heart of a cat beats twice as fast as that of a human heart; about 110 to 140 beats per minute

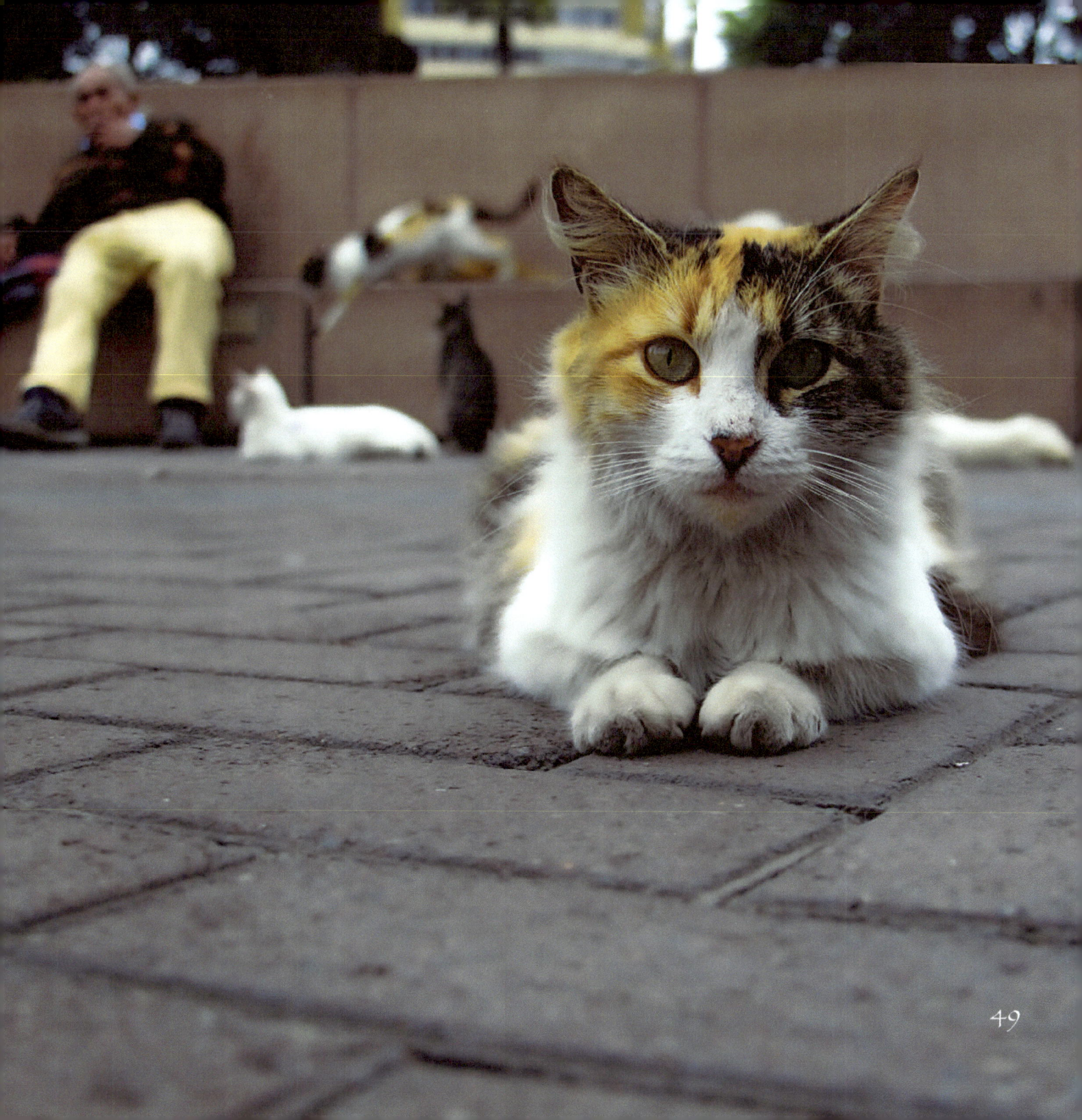

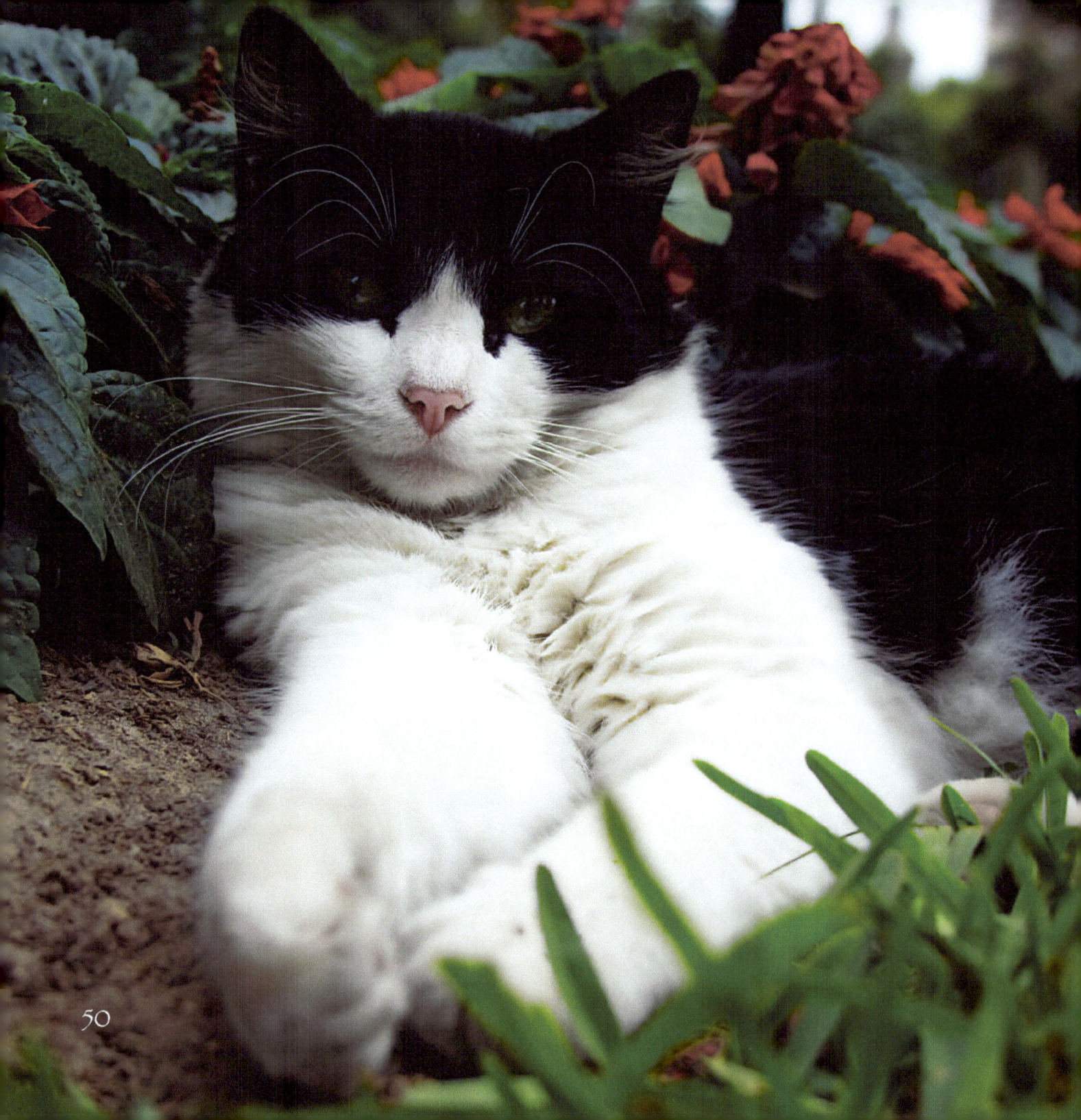

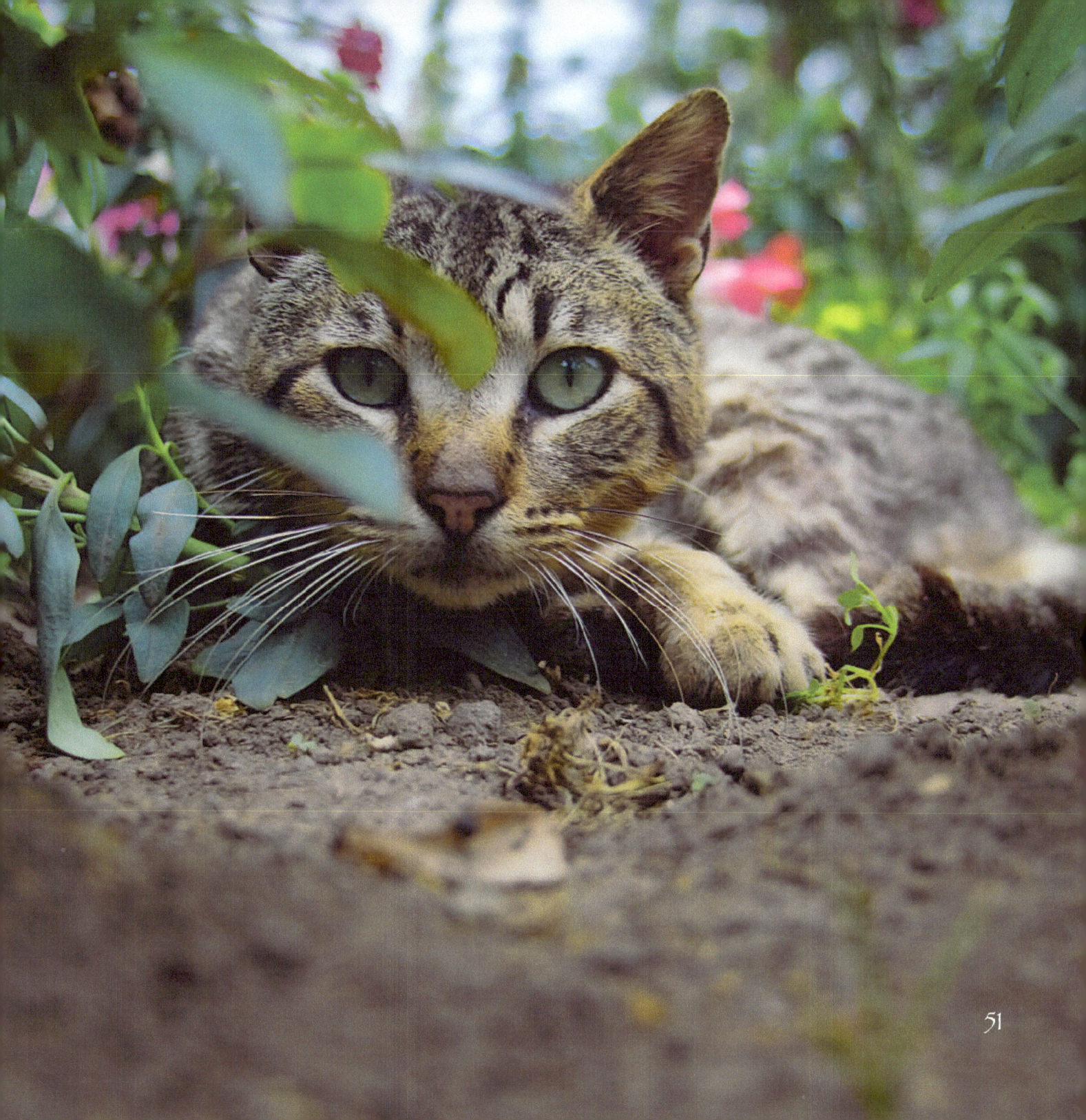

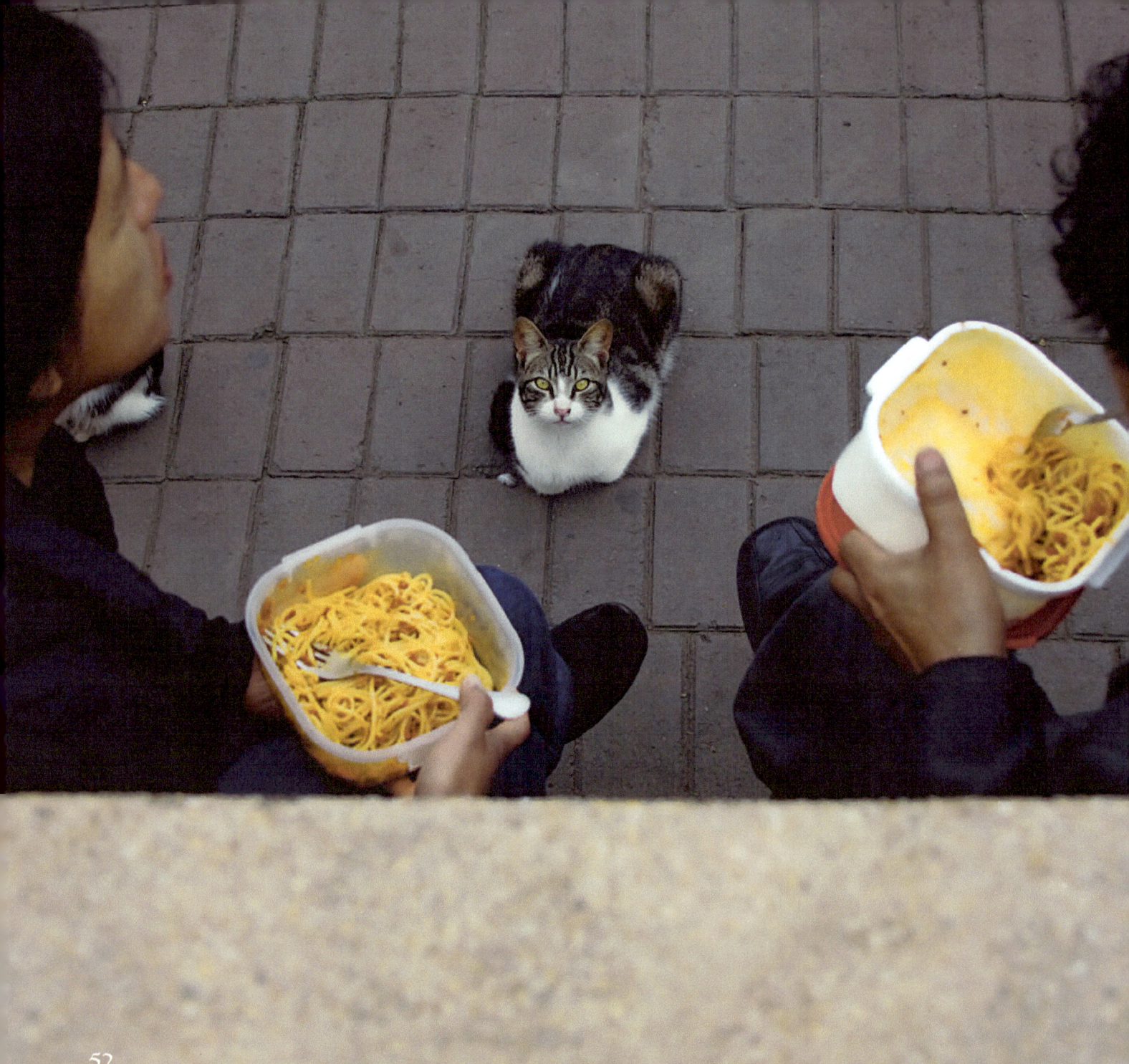

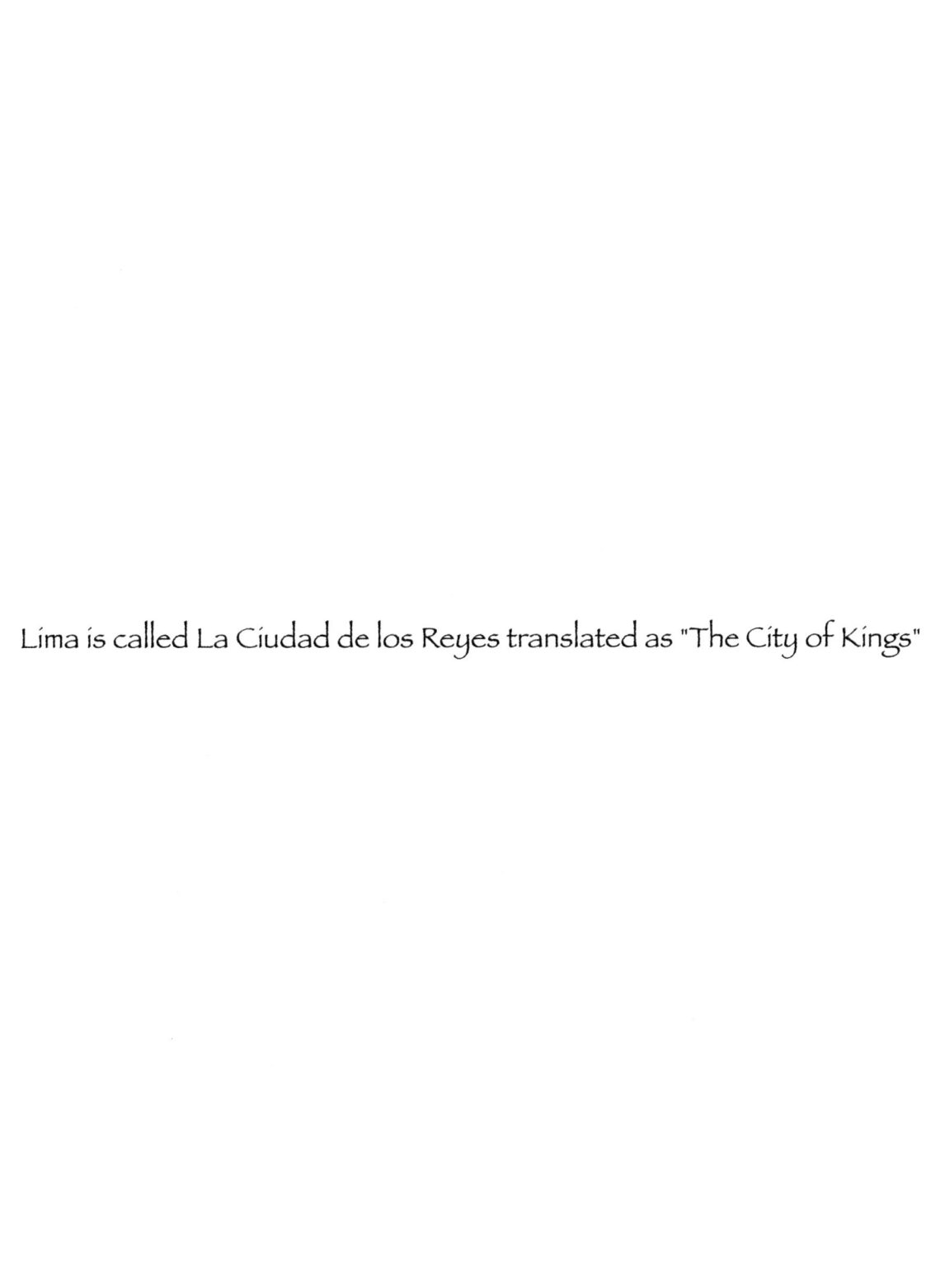

Lima is called La Ciudad de los Reyes translated as "The City of Kings"

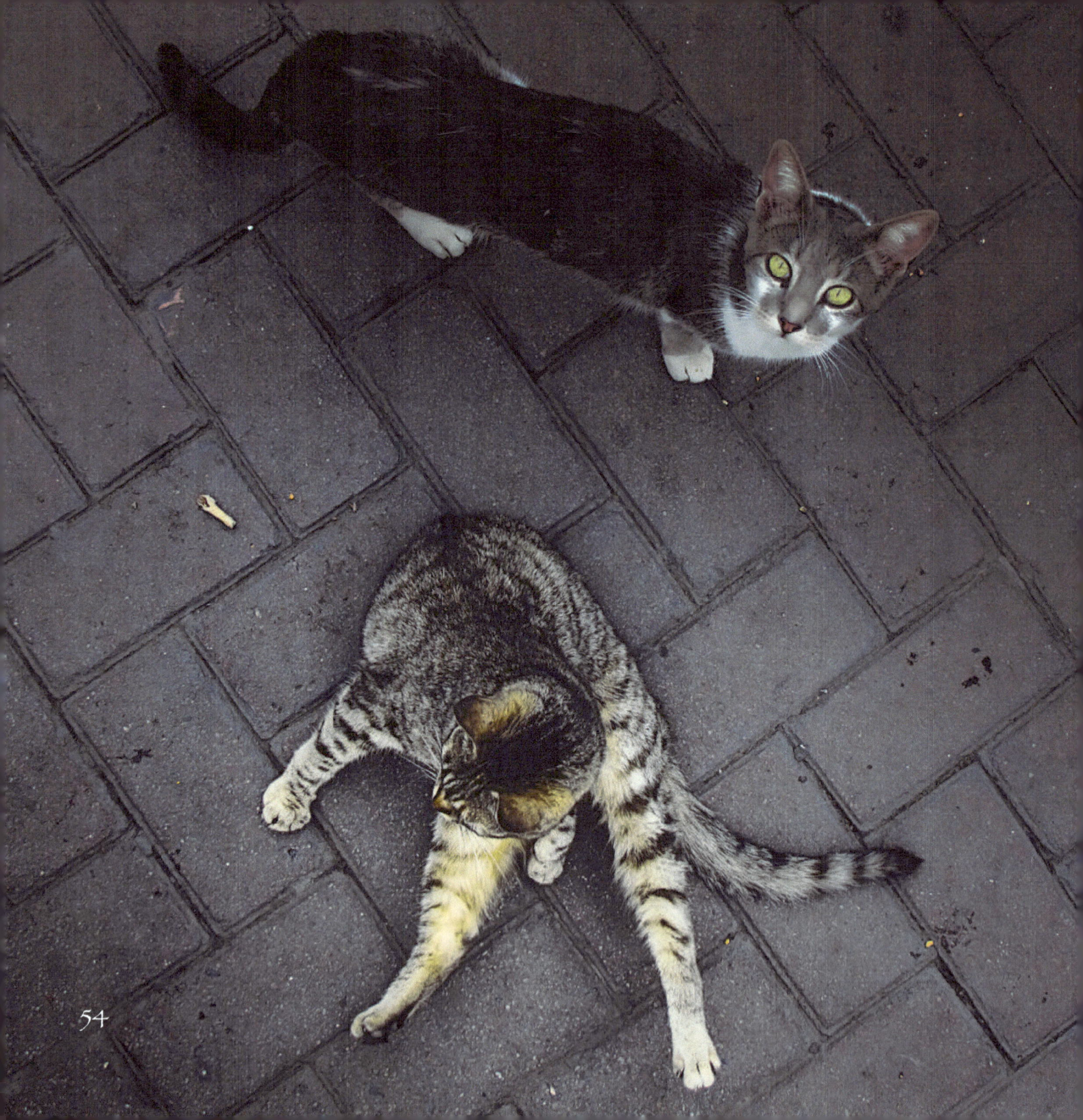

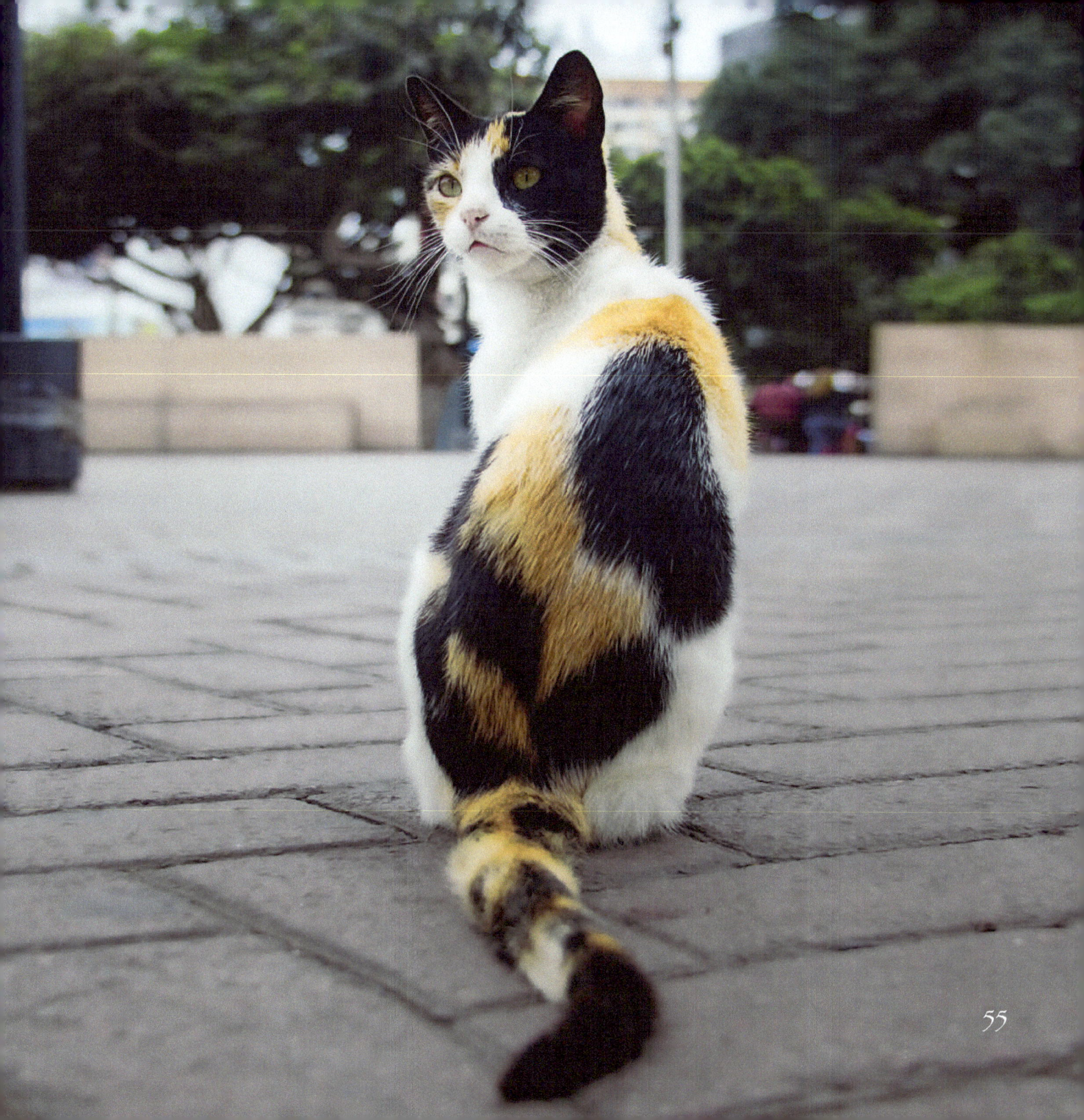

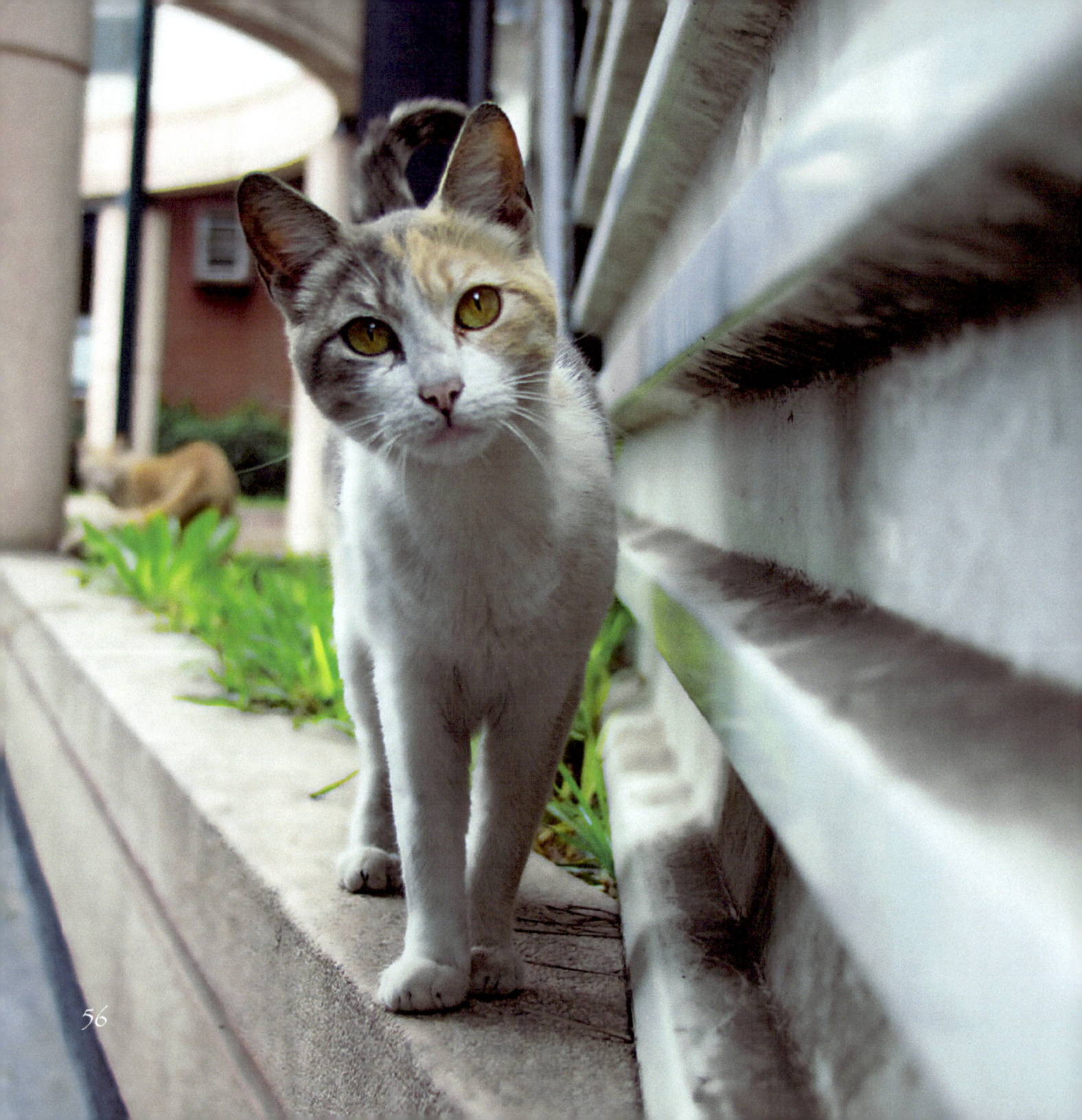

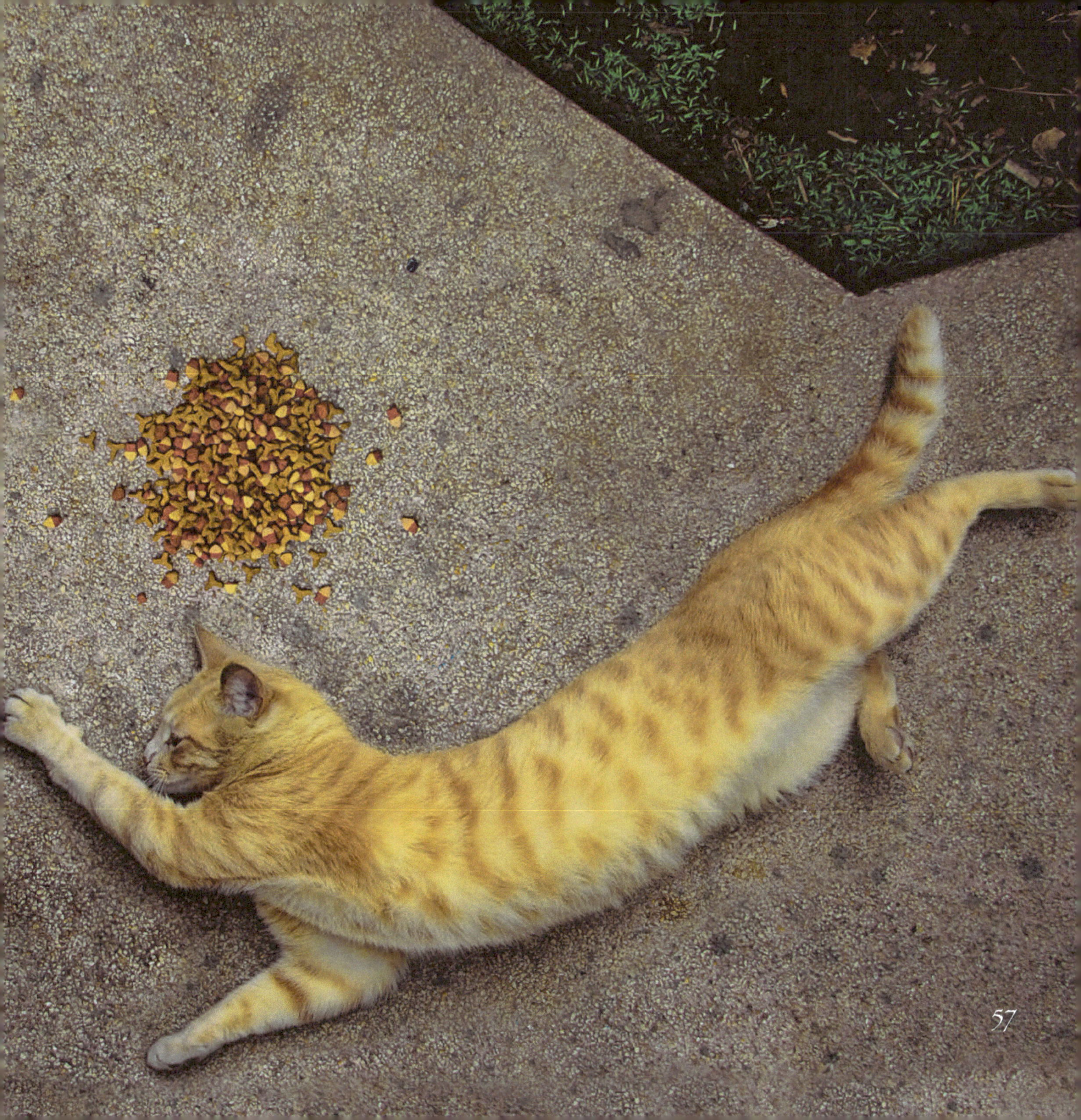

Cat haters are called ailurophobes

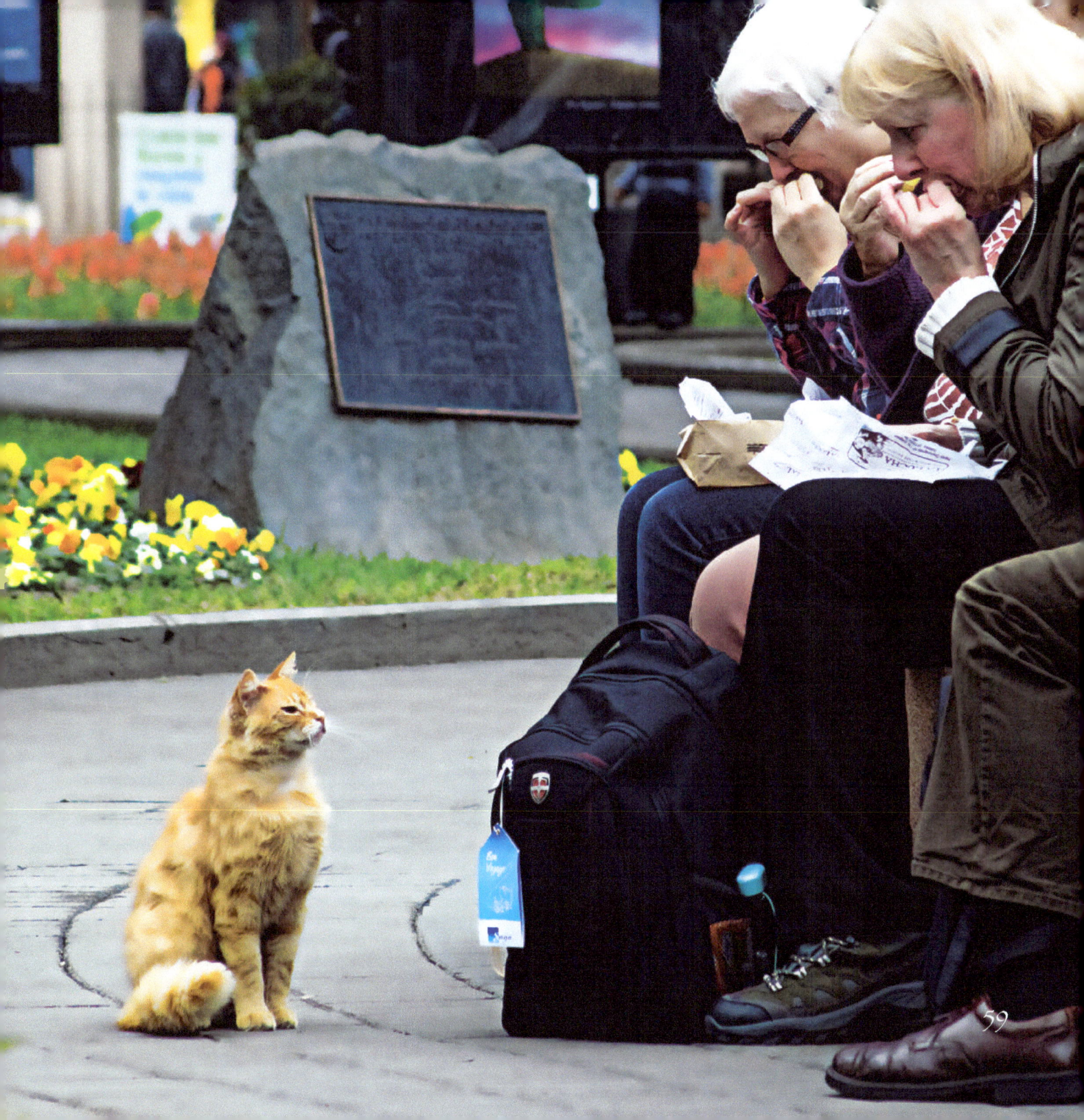

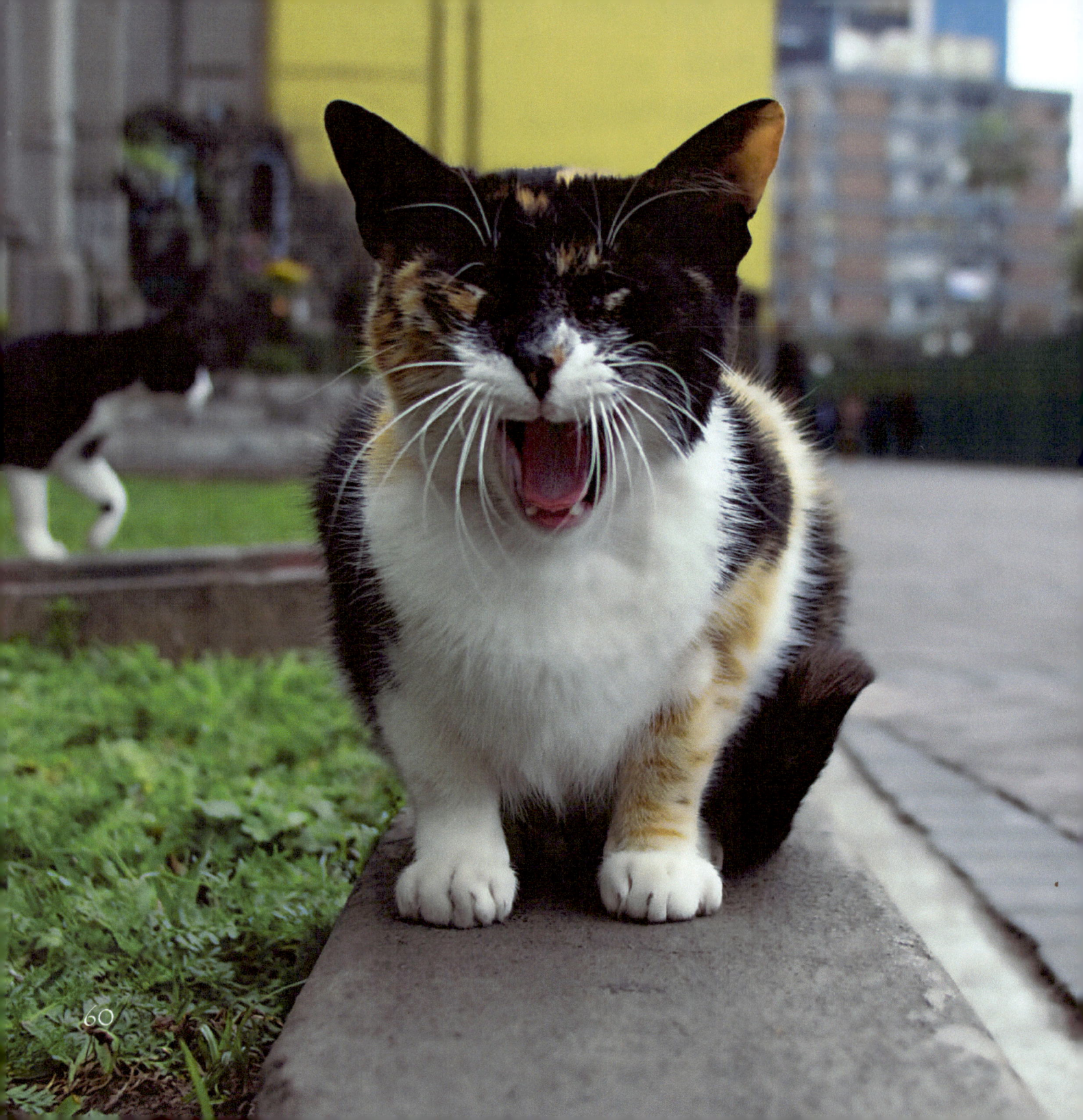

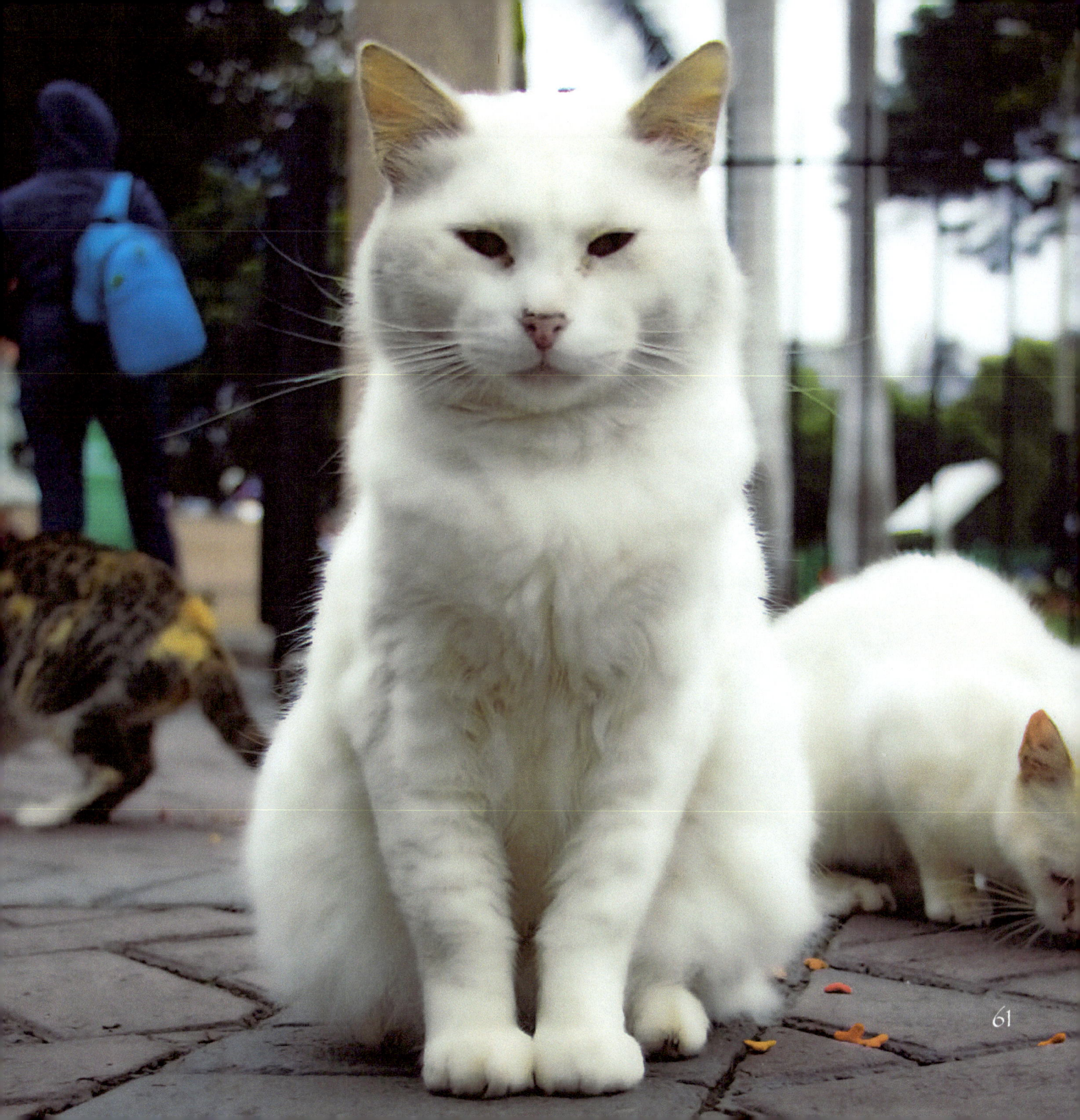

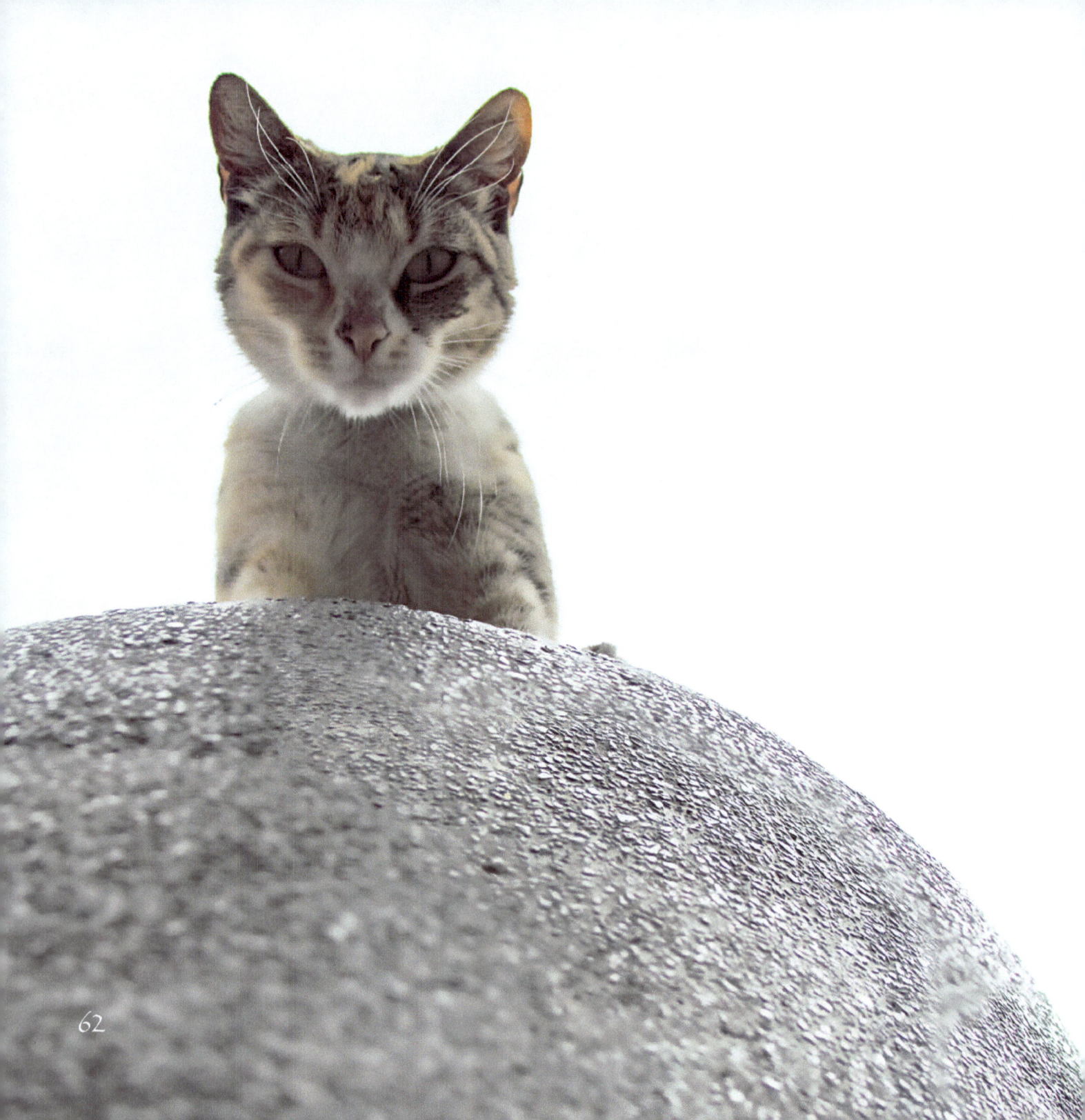

Lima occupies an area measuring 1,677 square miles and has a coastline that extends for 49miles

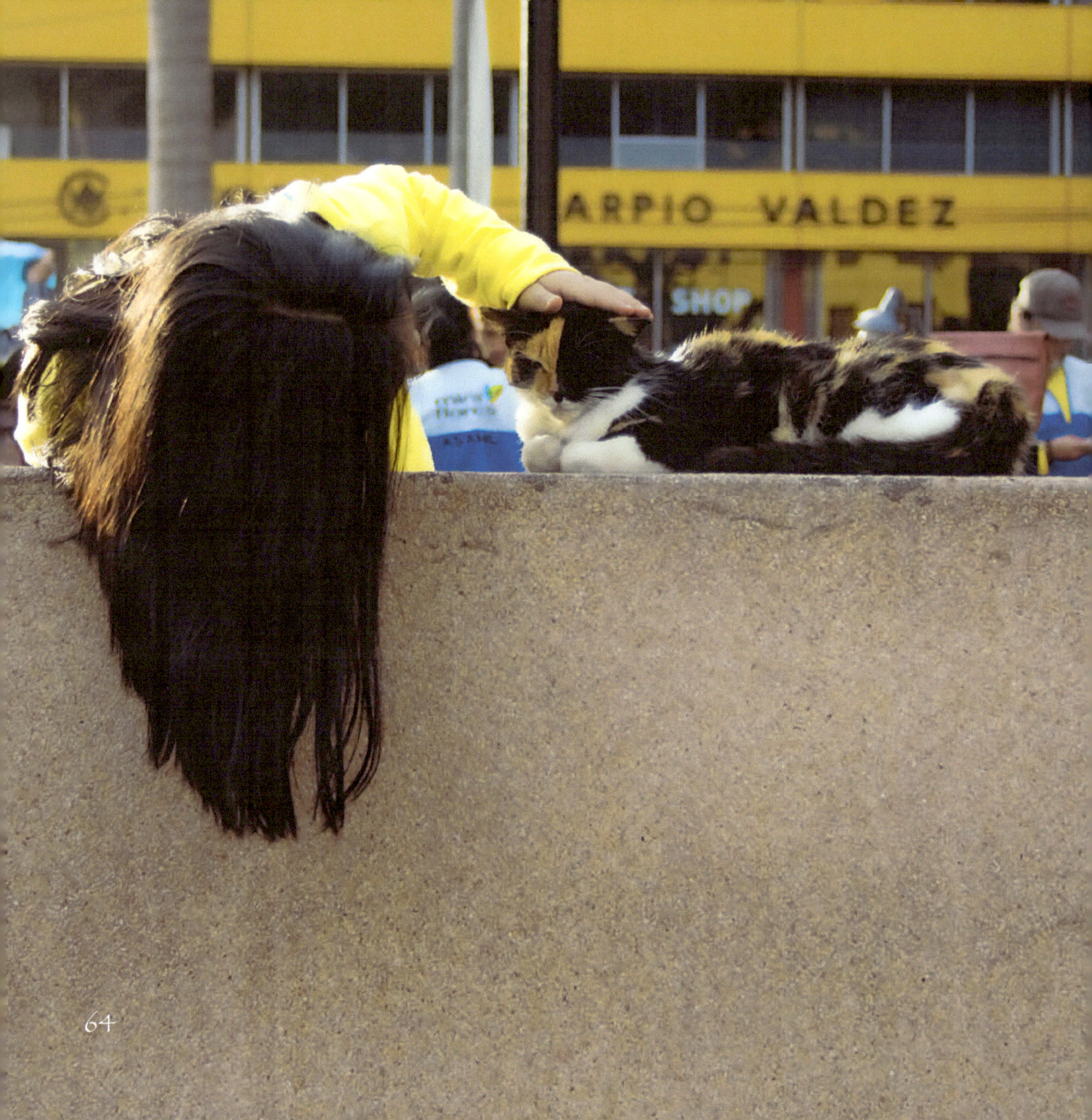

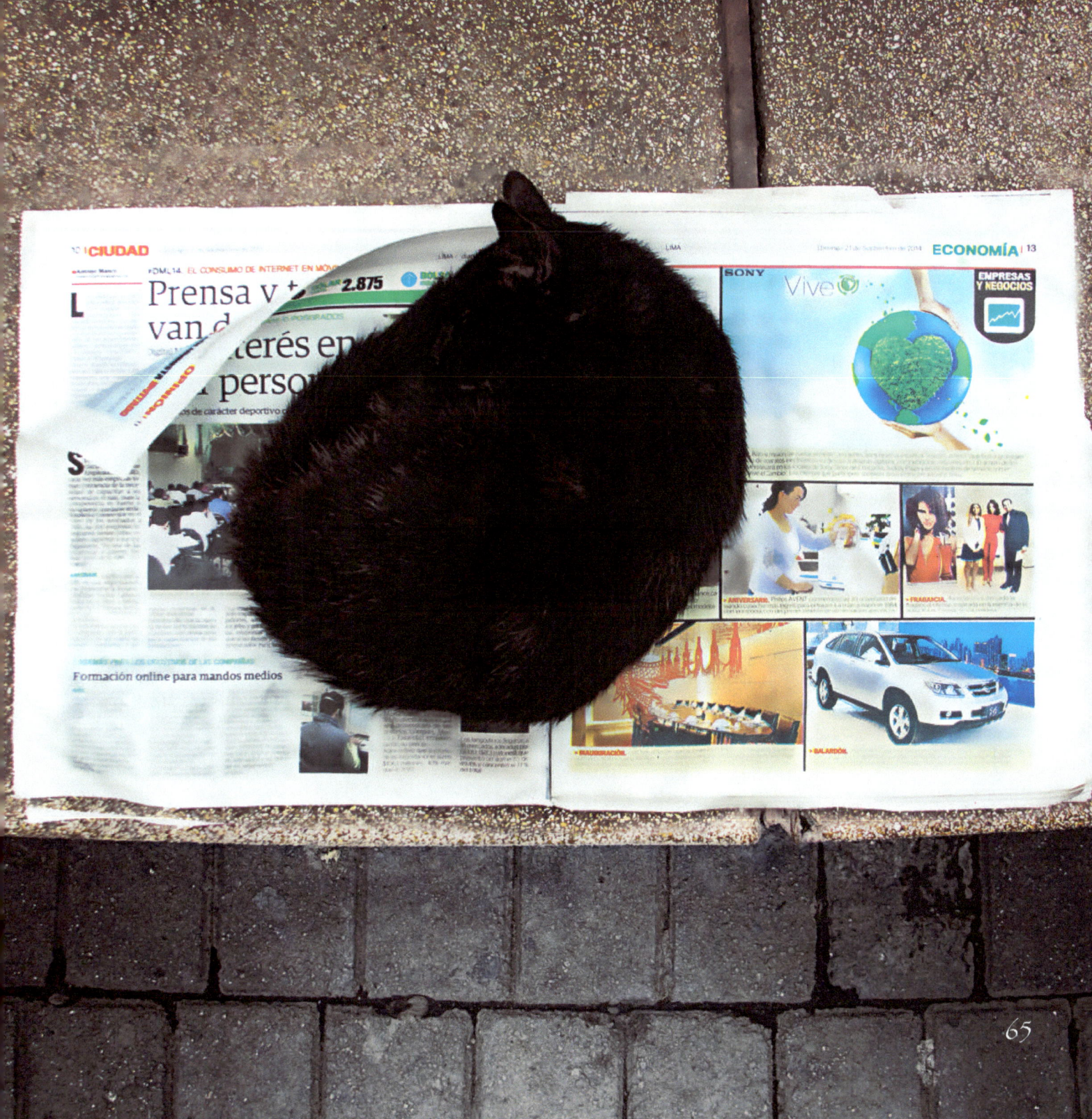

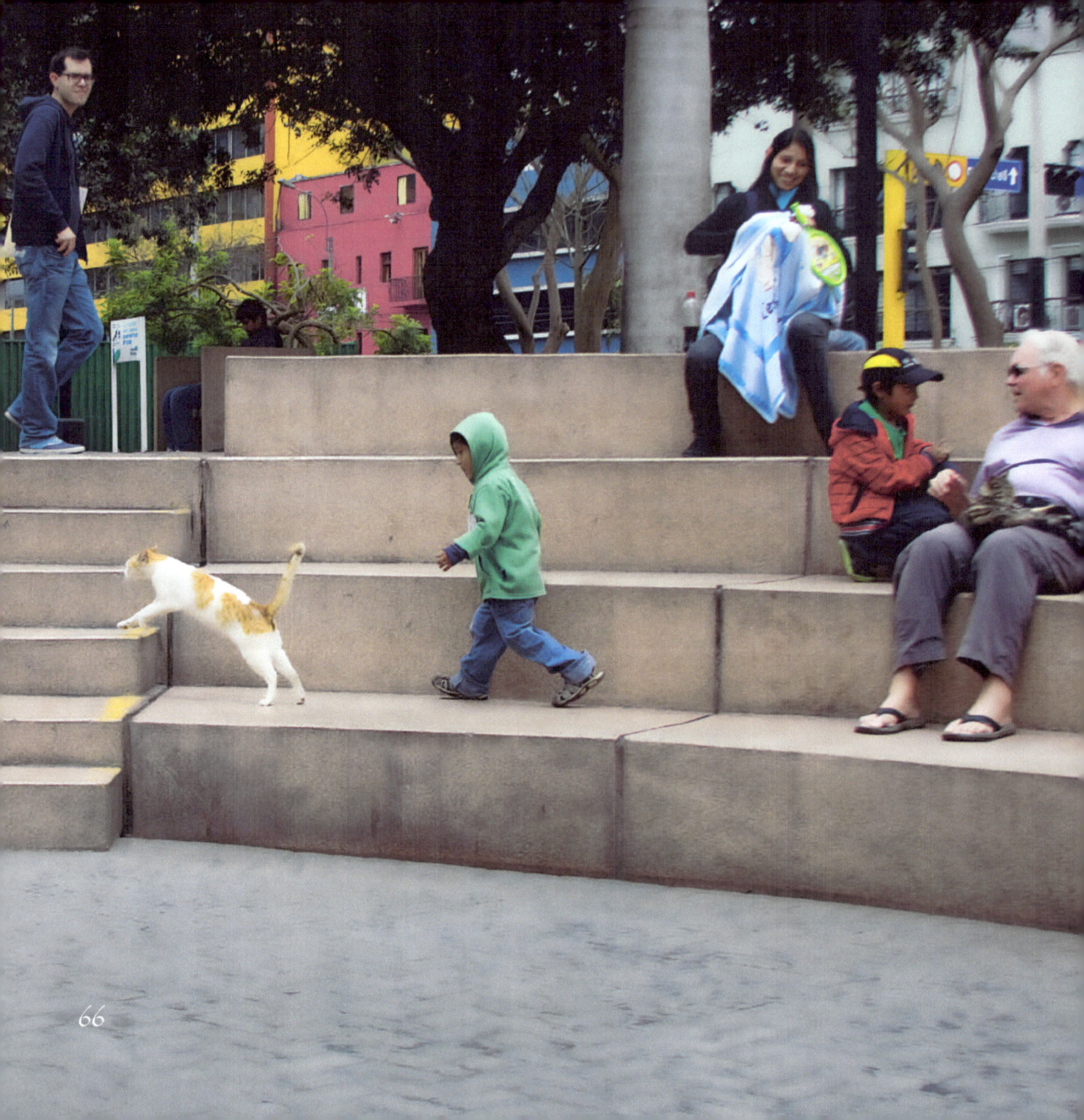

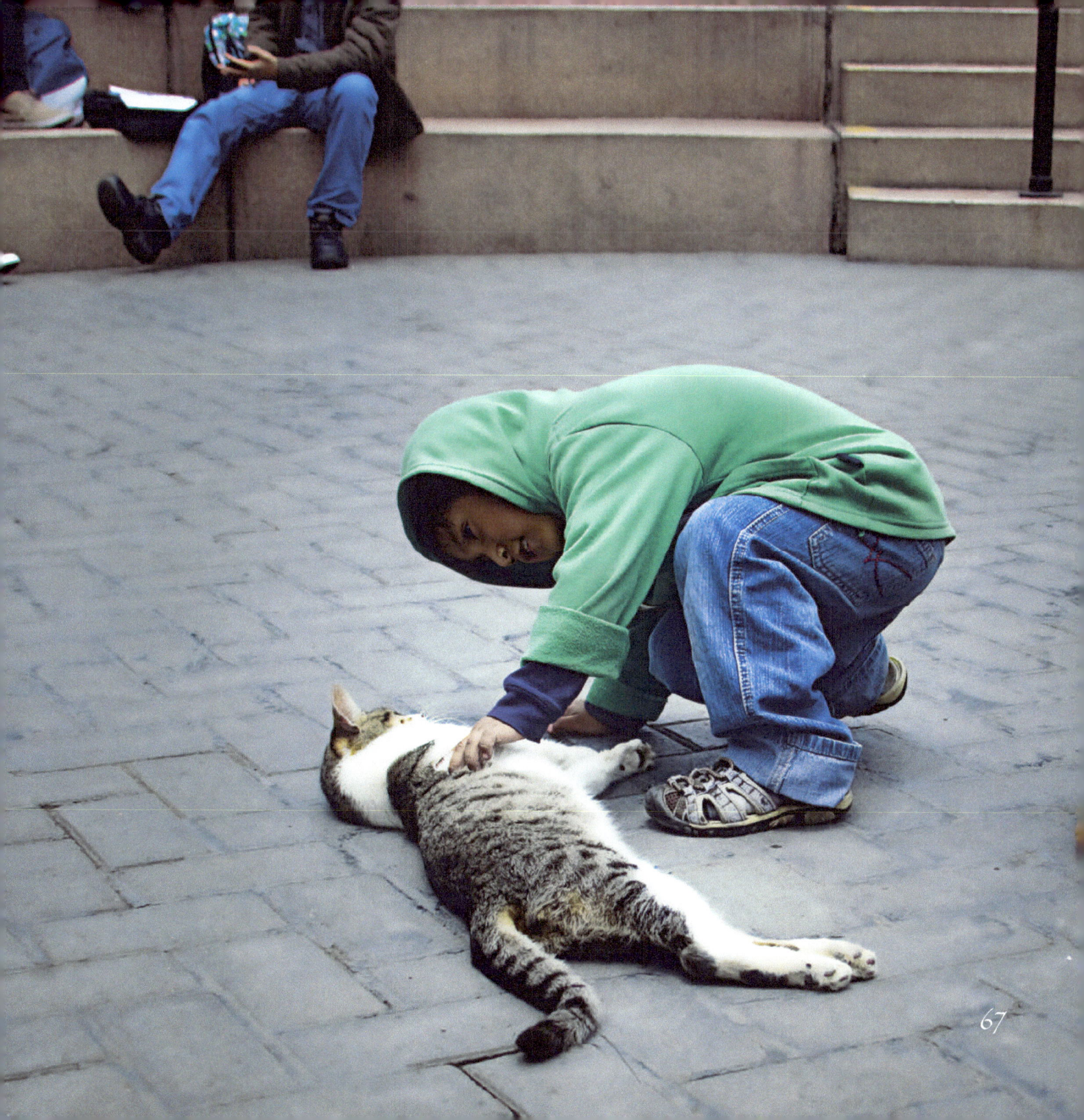

Newborn kittens have closed ear canals that don't begin to open for nine days

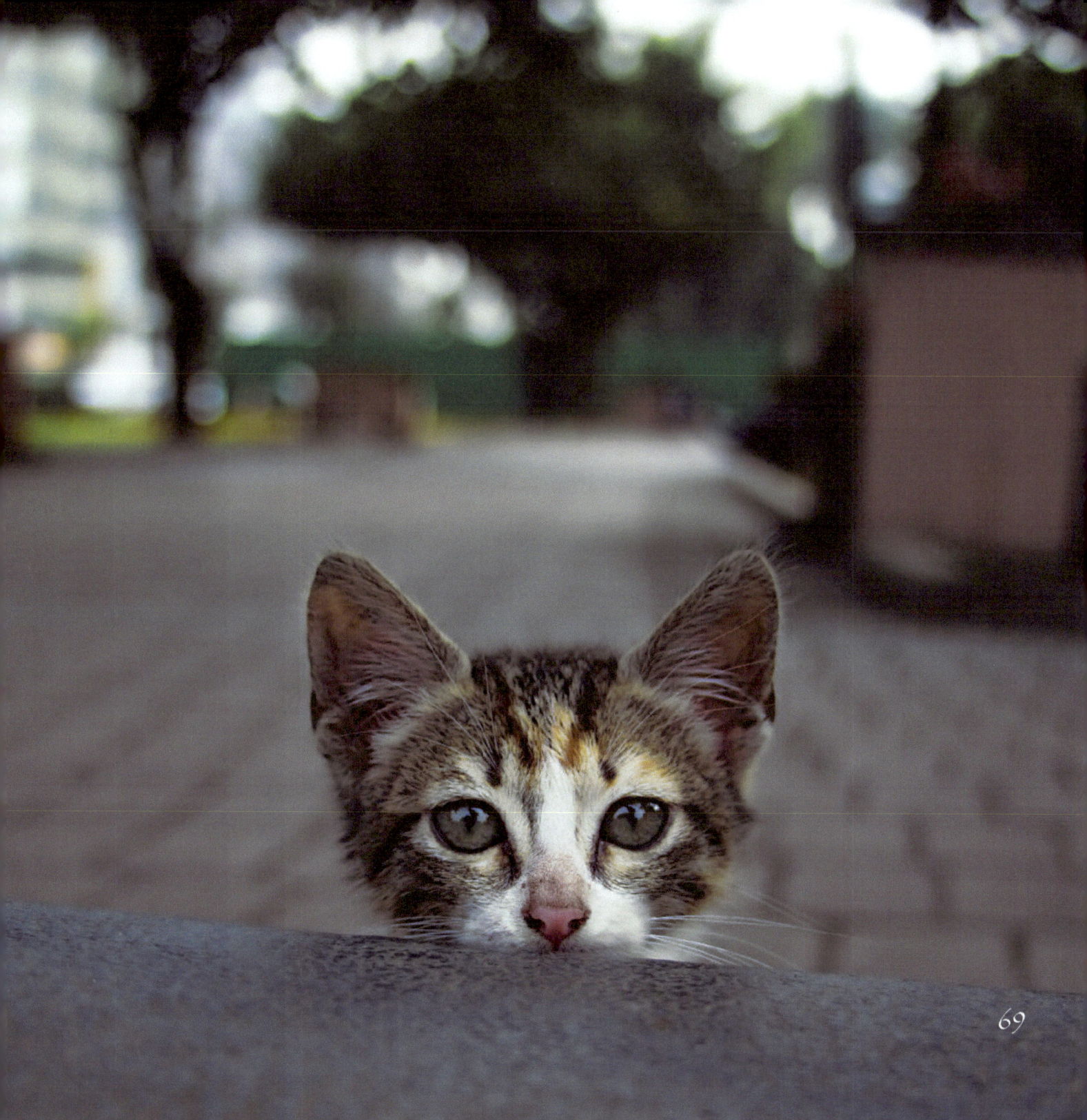

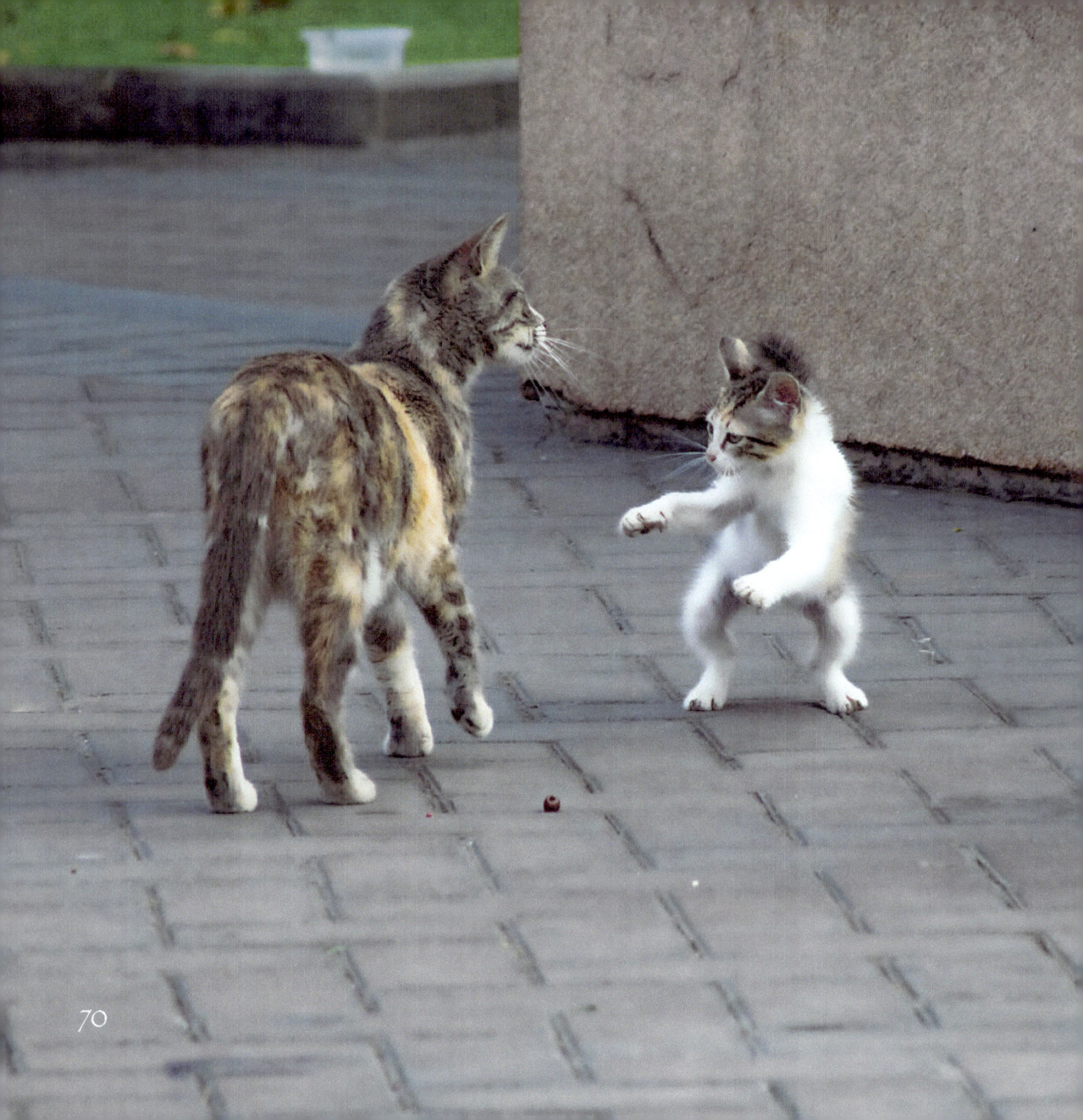

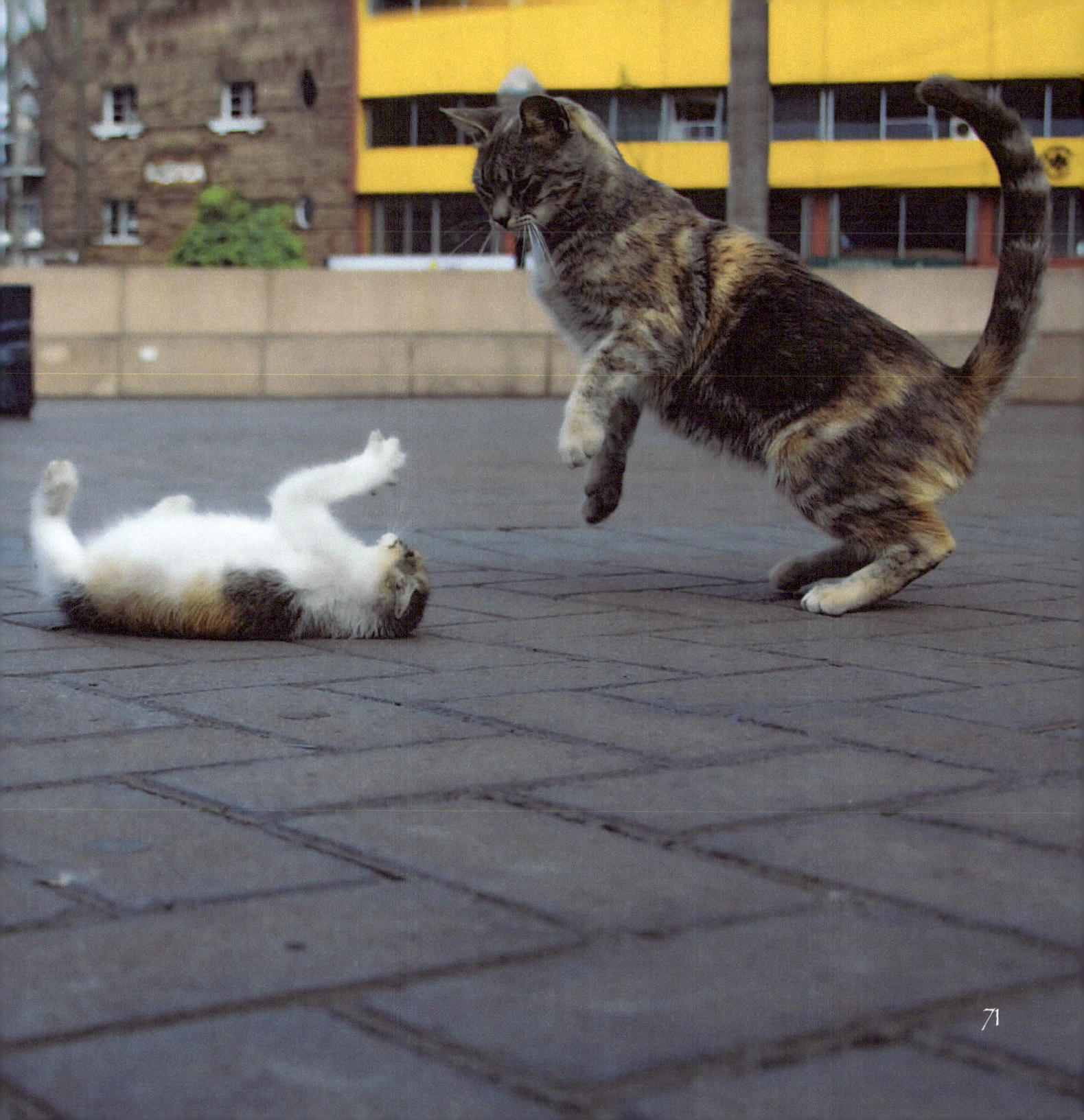

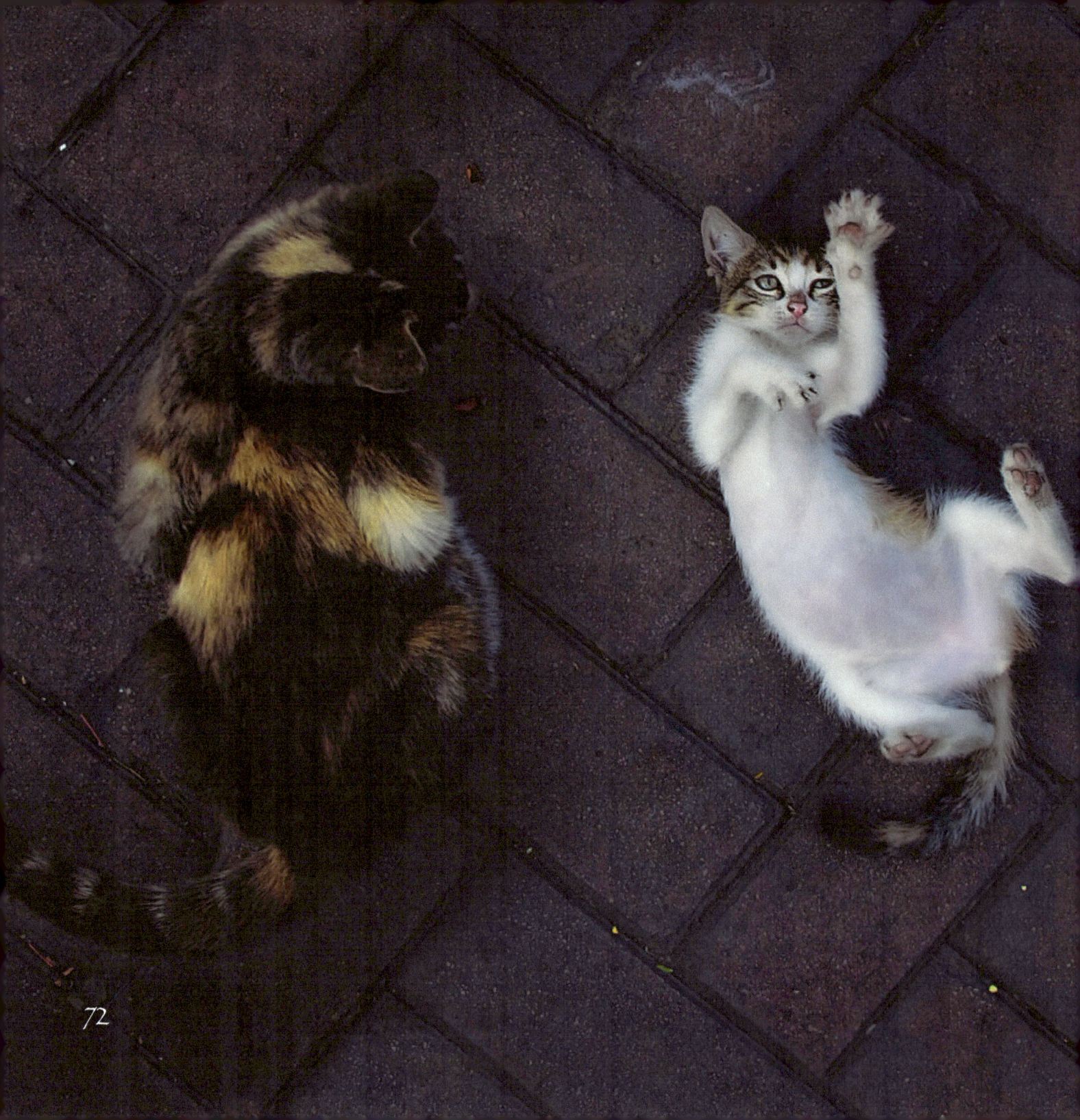

The Spanish conquistador Francisco Pizarro founded Lima on January 18, 1535

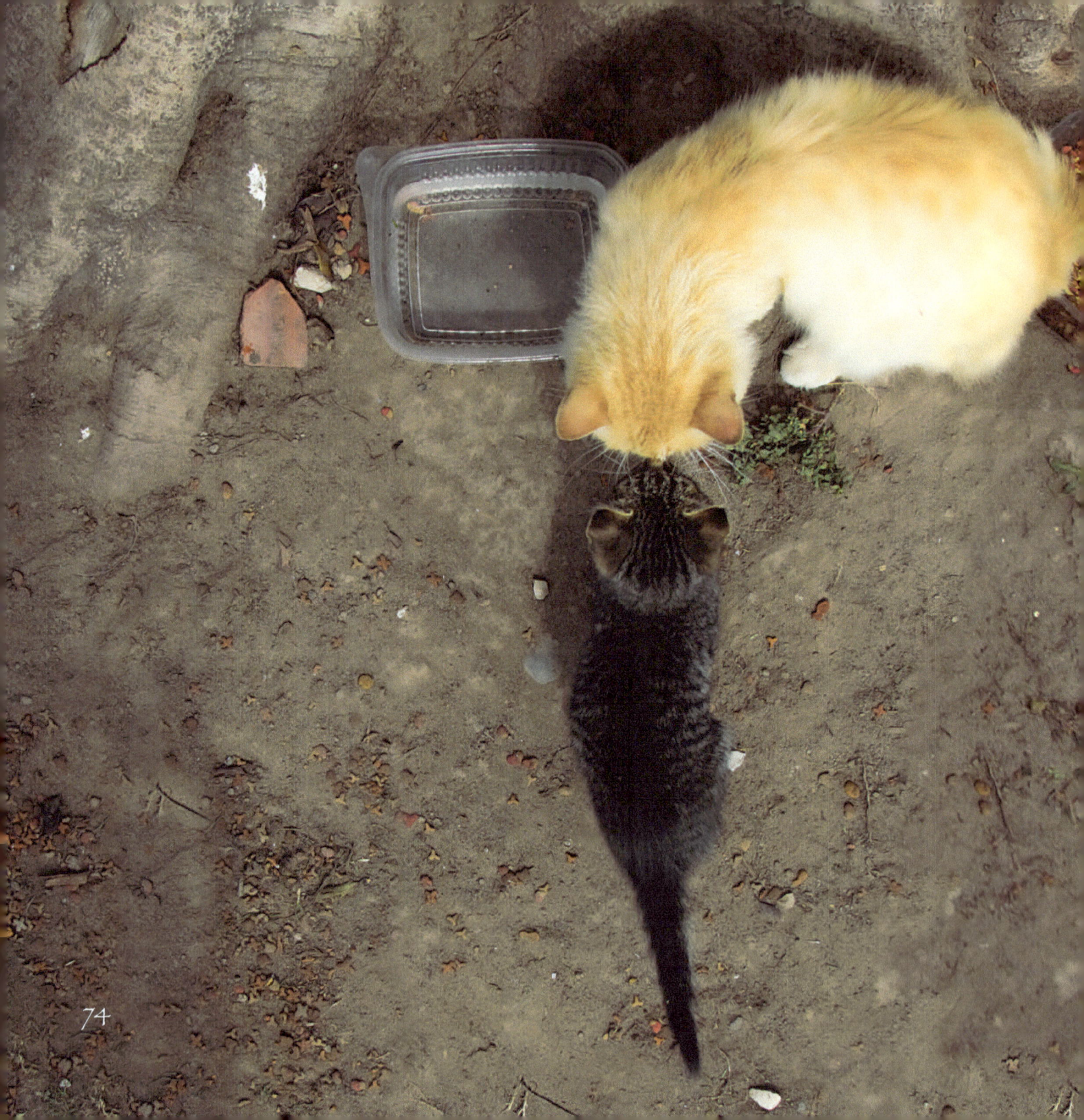

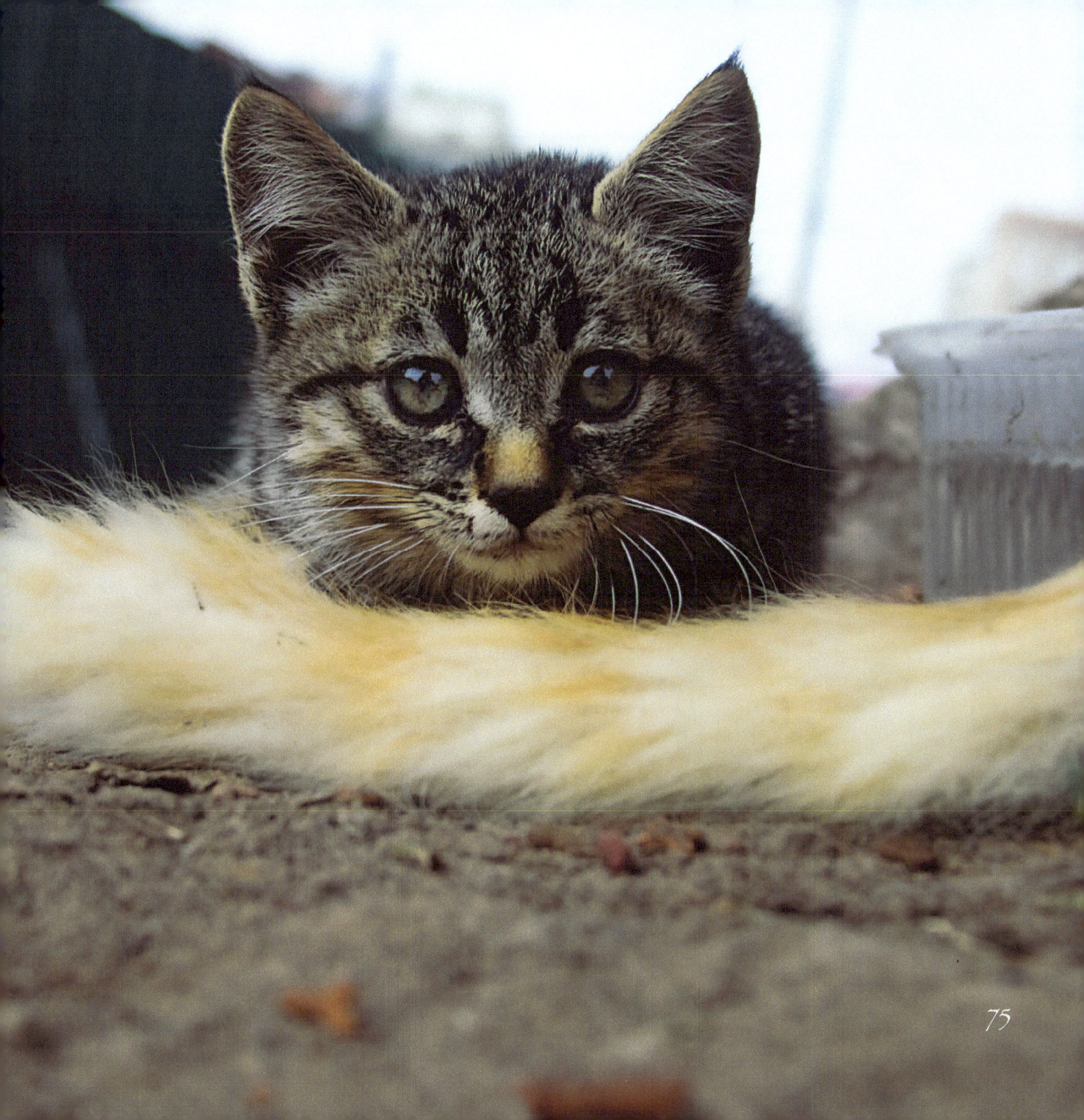

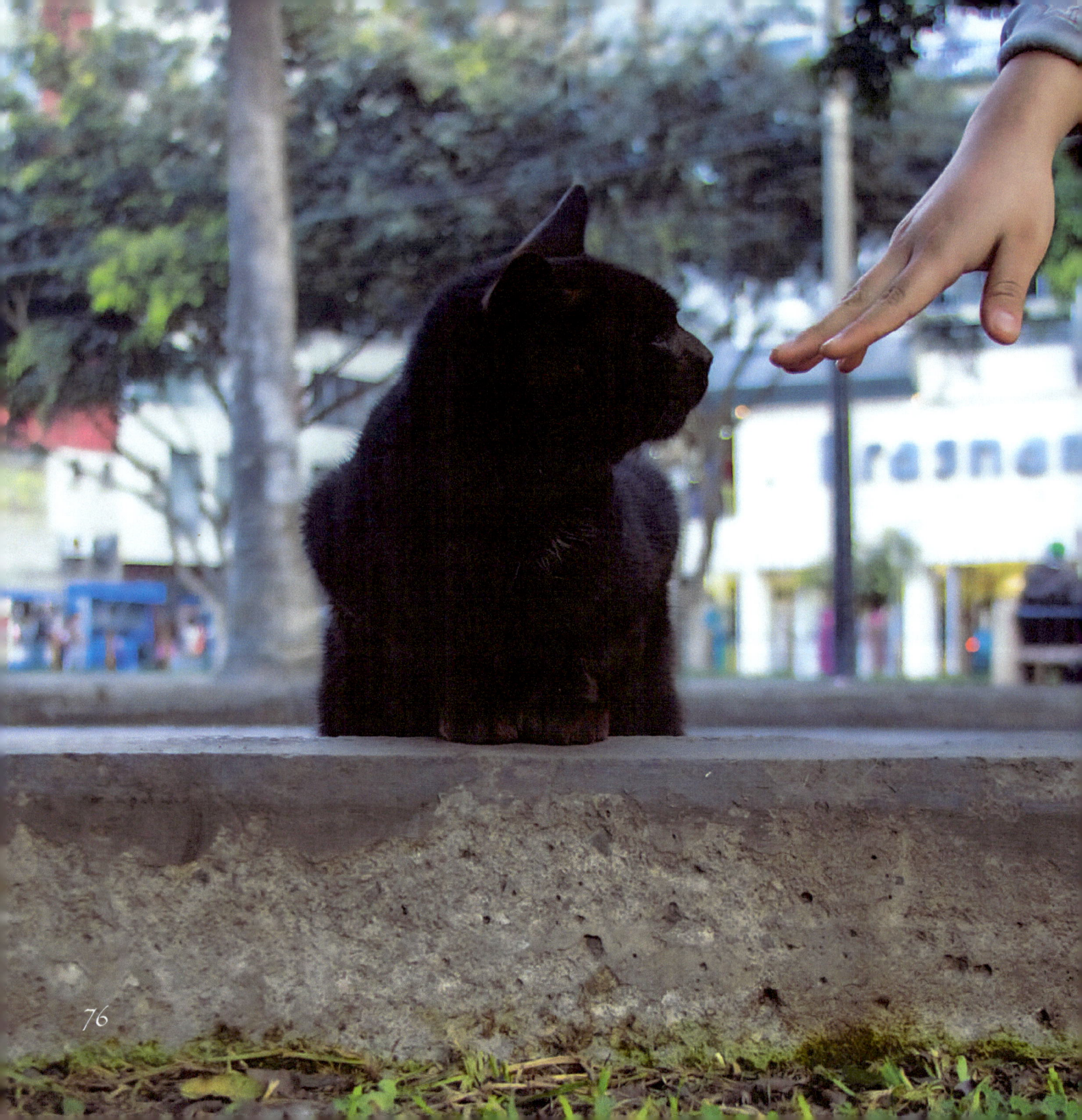

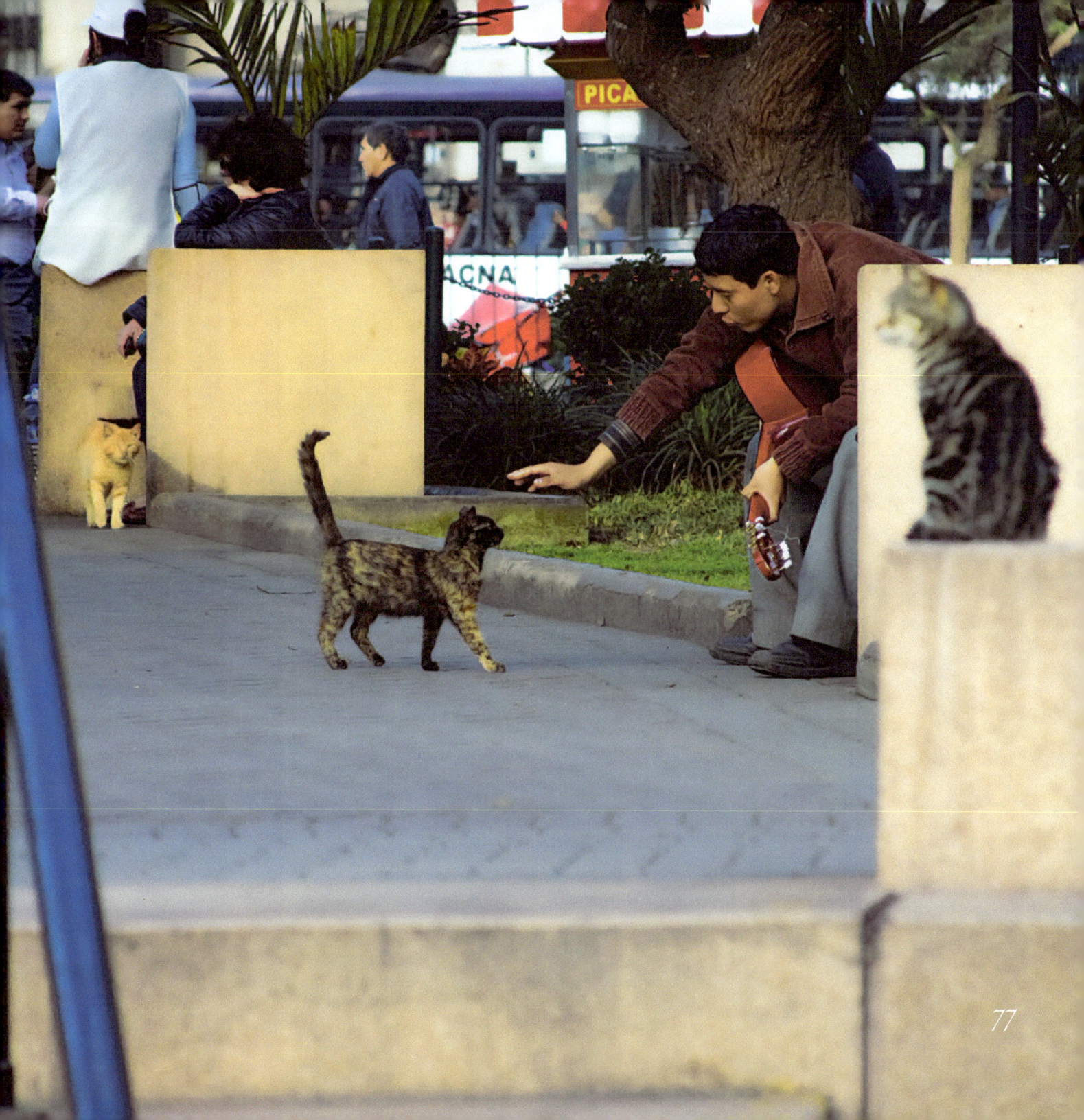

The Ragdoll is the largest domestic breed of cat. Males can range from 12 to 20 pounds while females are 10 to 15 pounds

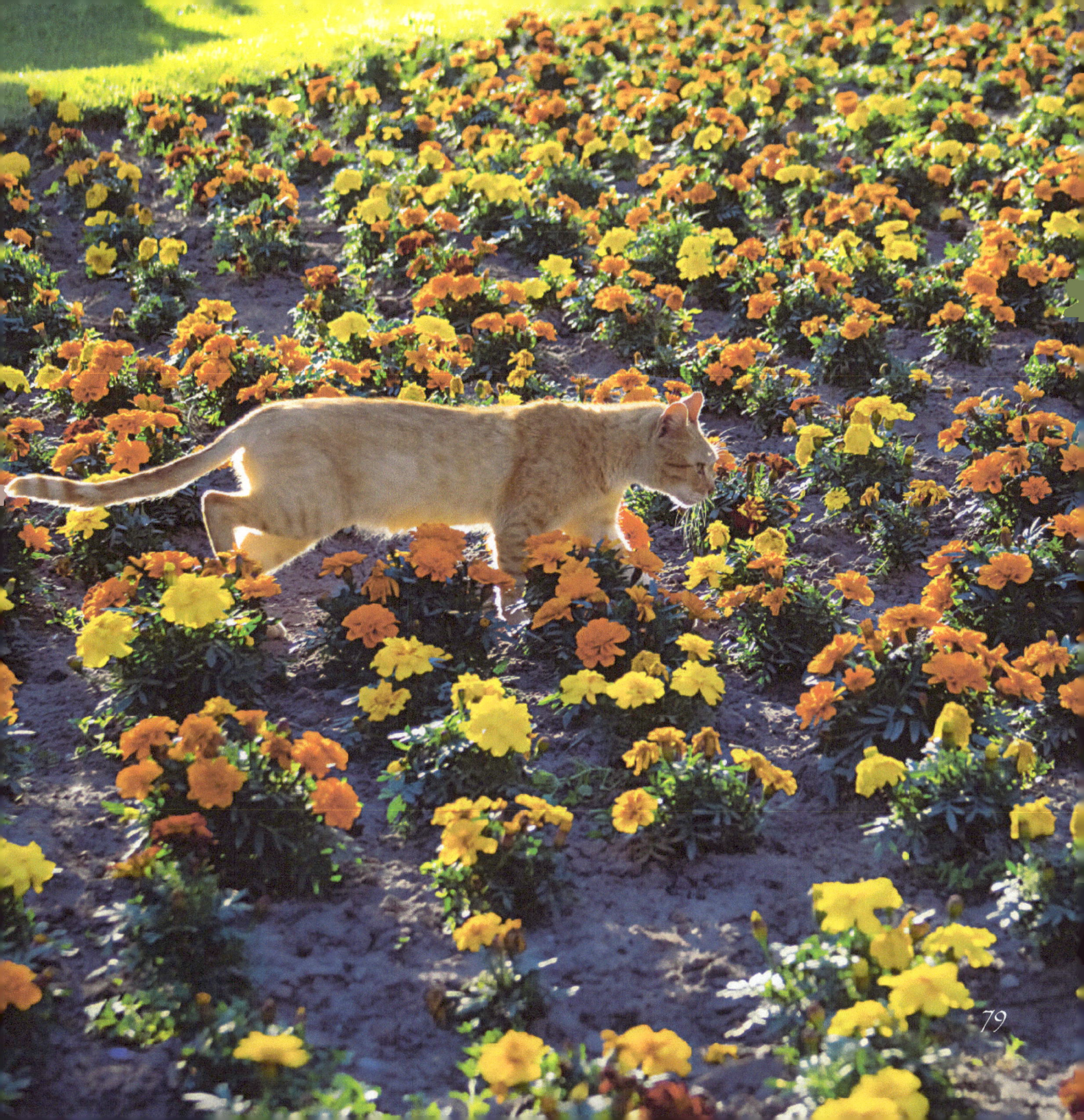

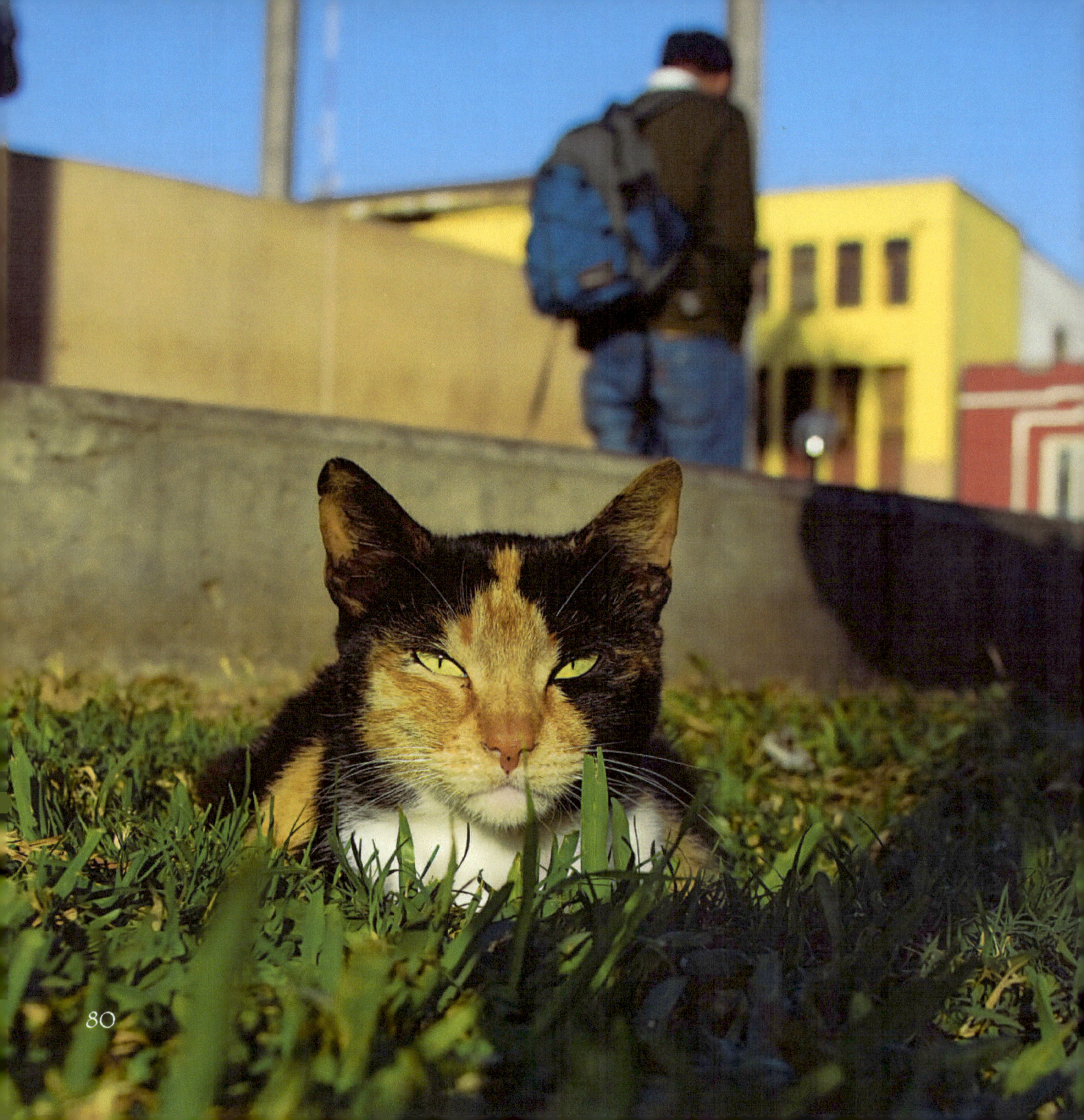

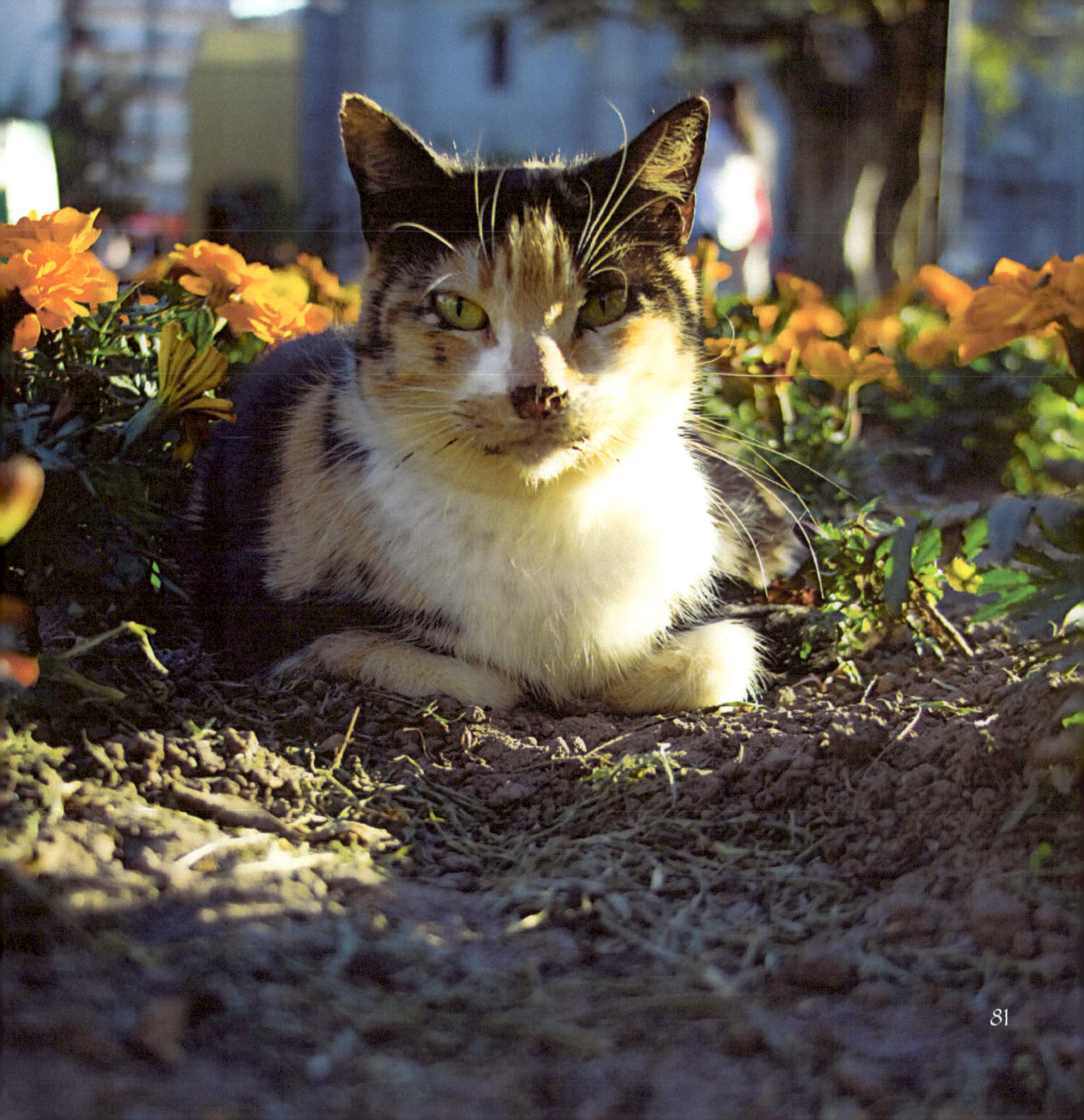

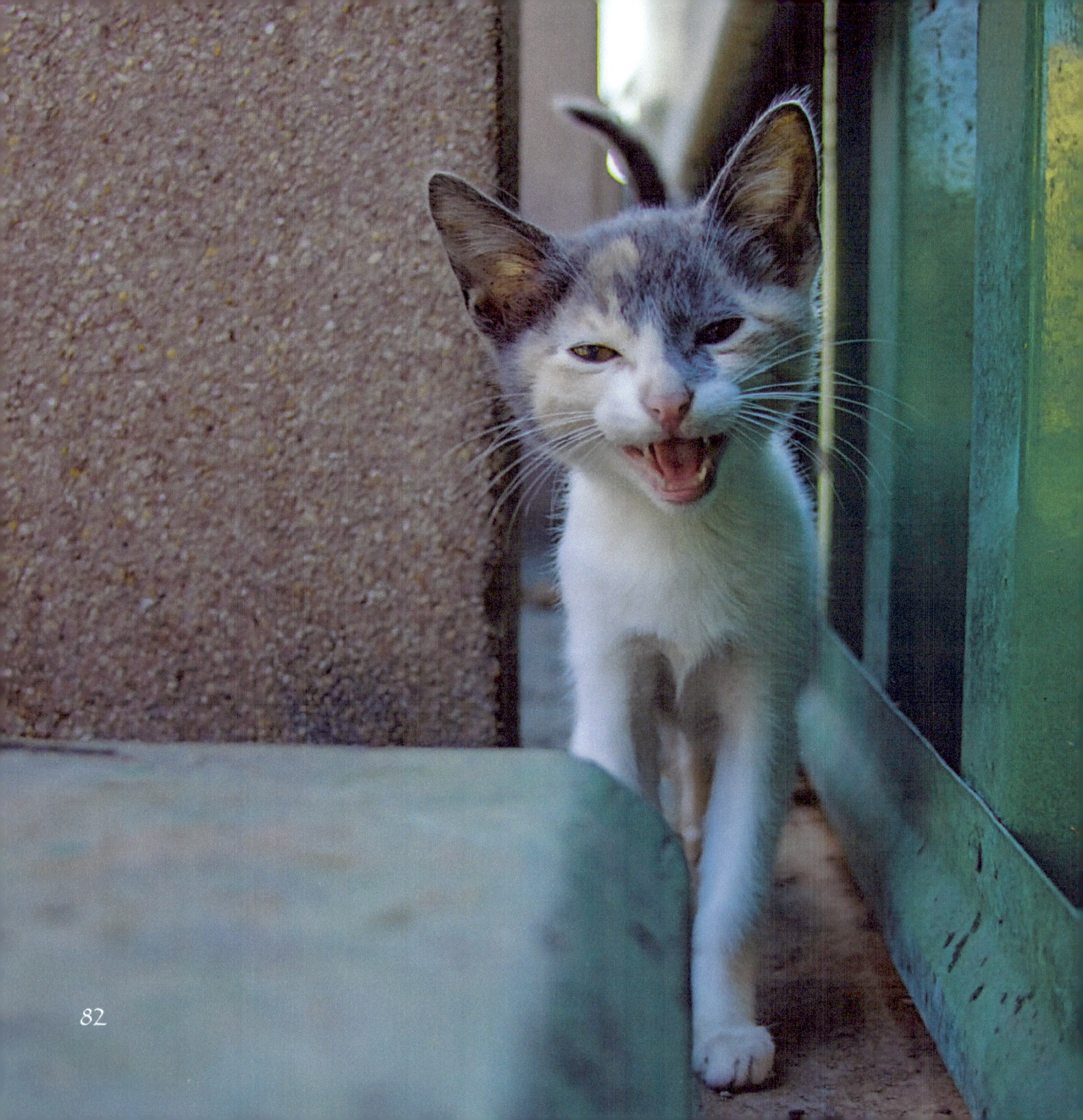

The Spanish Crown ruled Lima for over 300 years

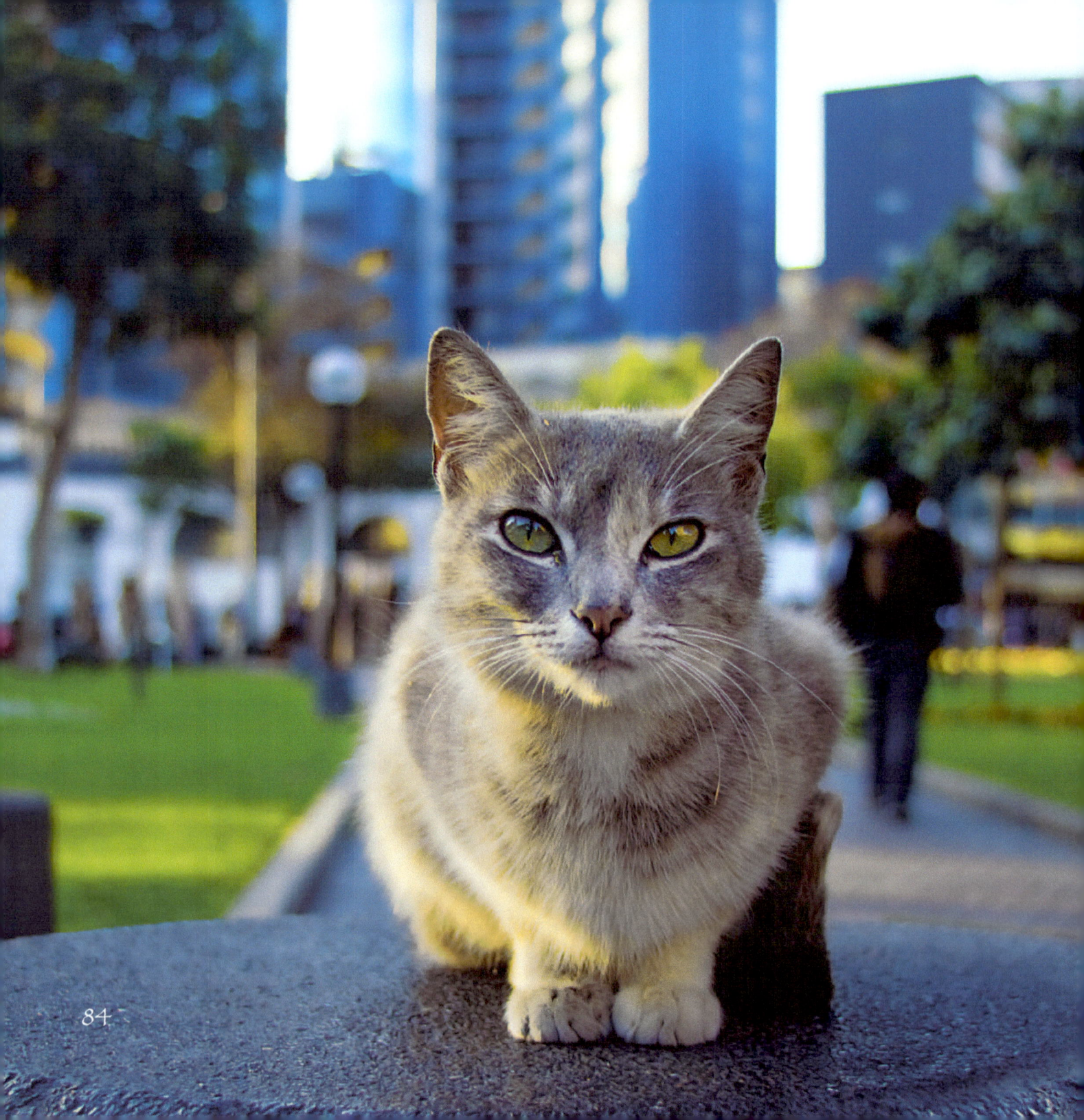

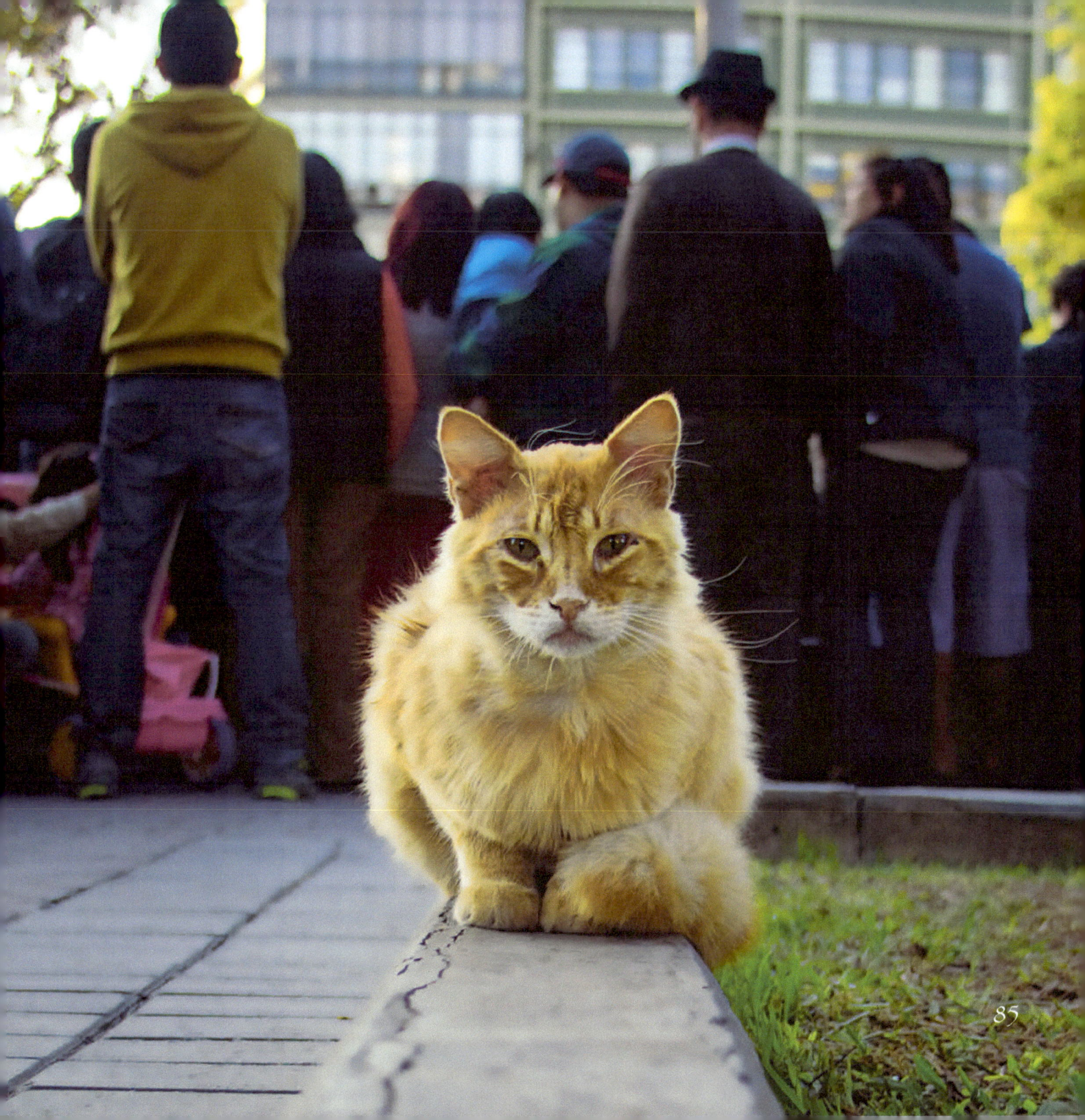

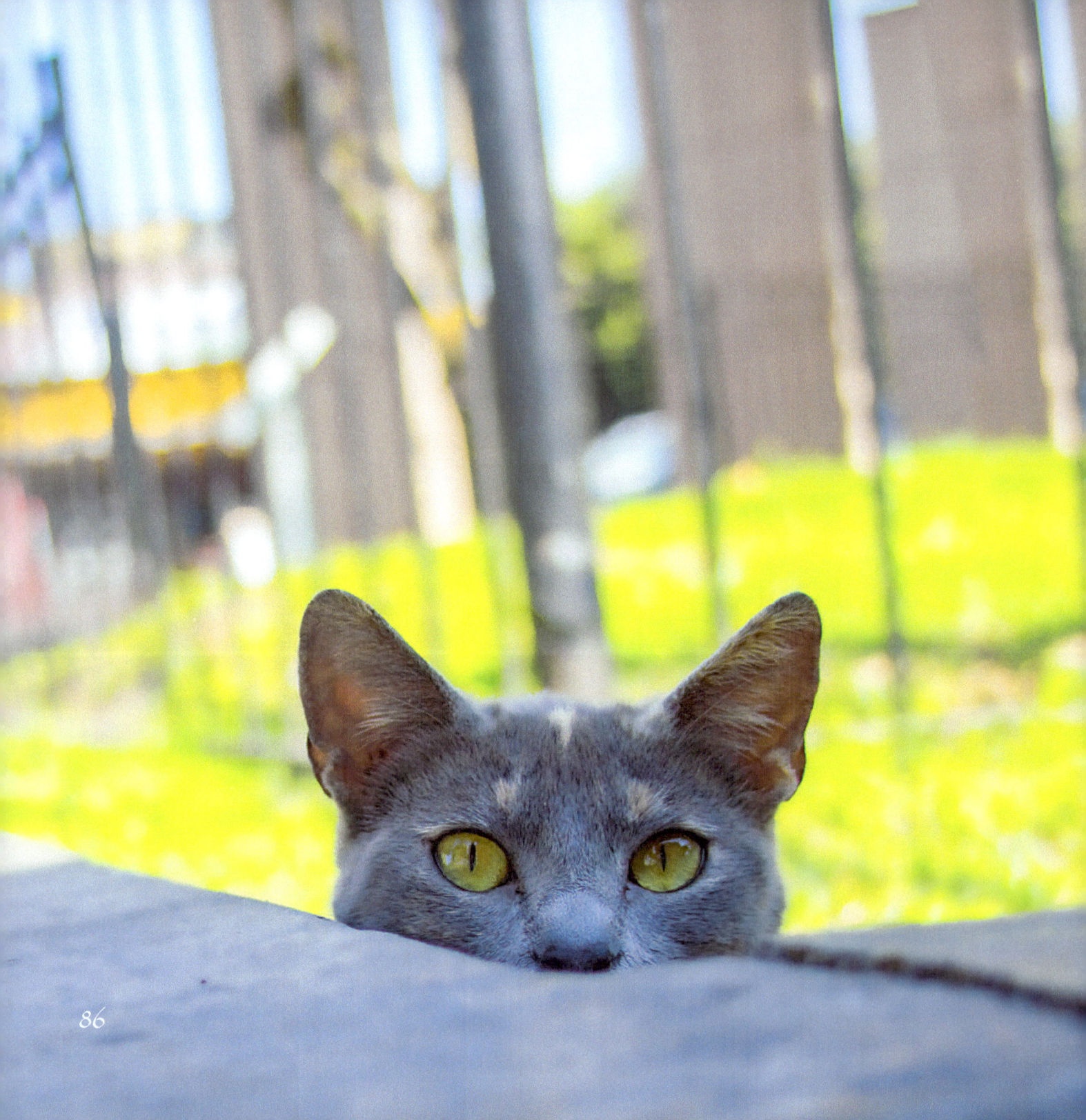

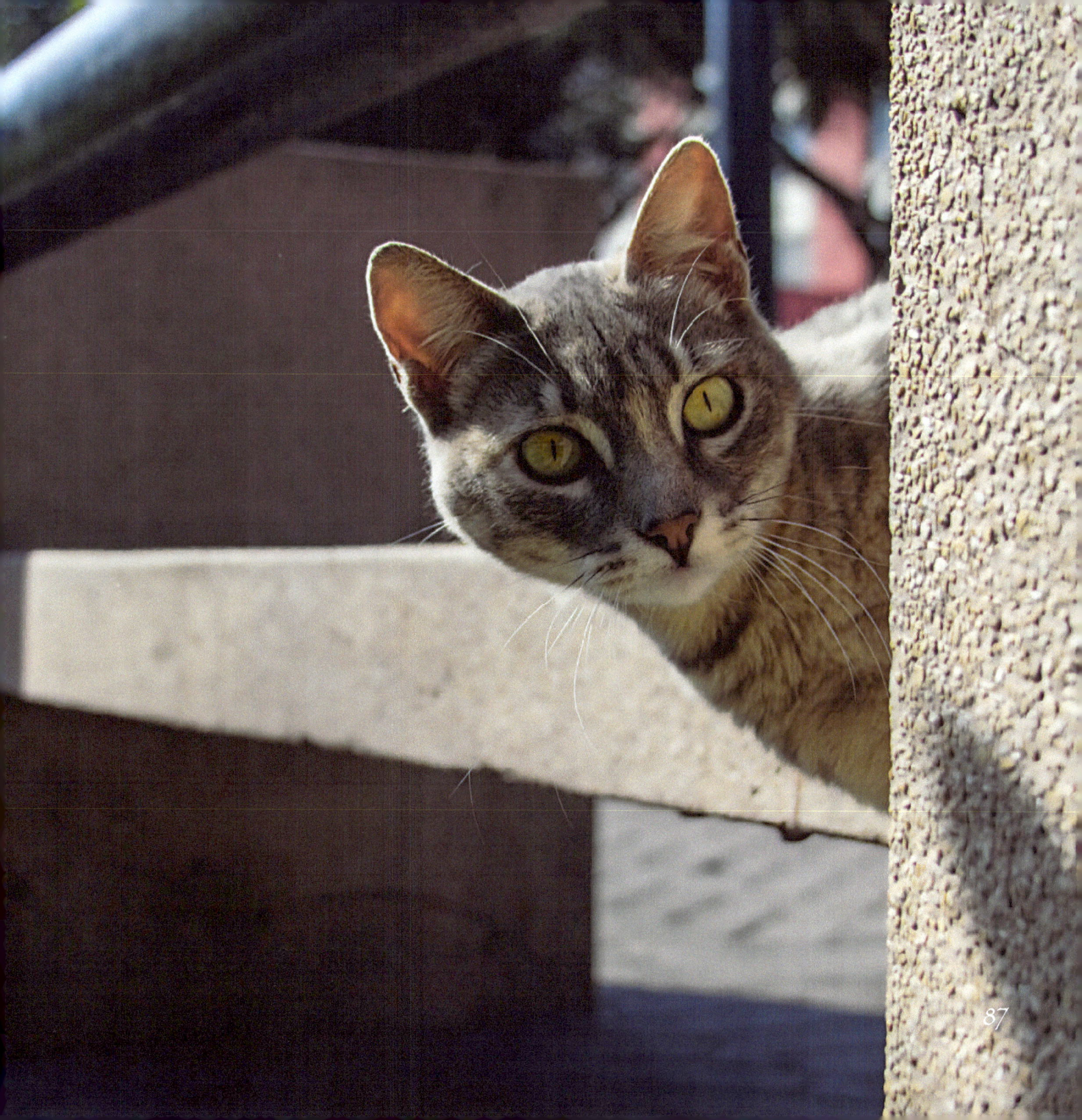

Cats purr around 26 cycles per second

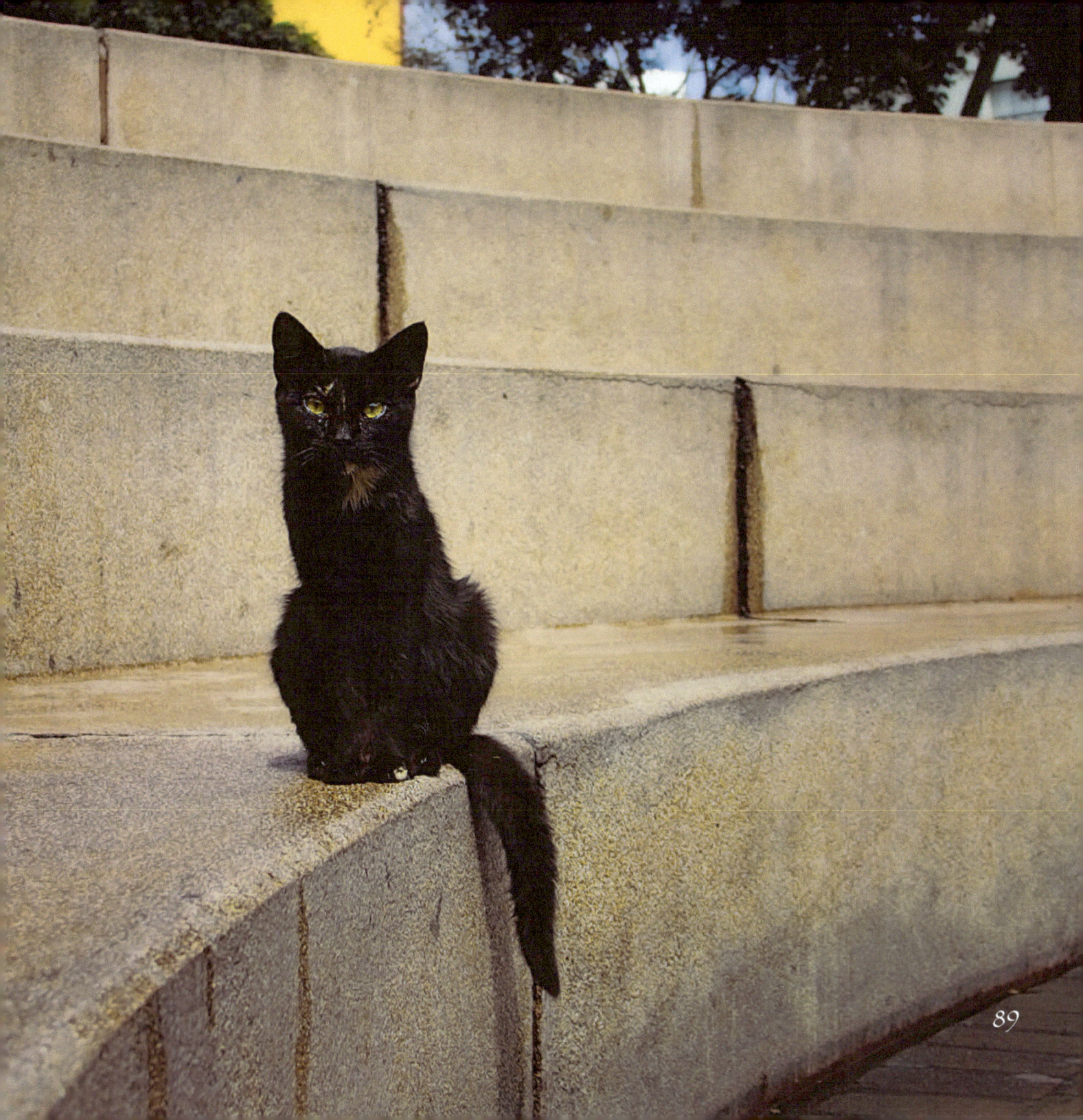

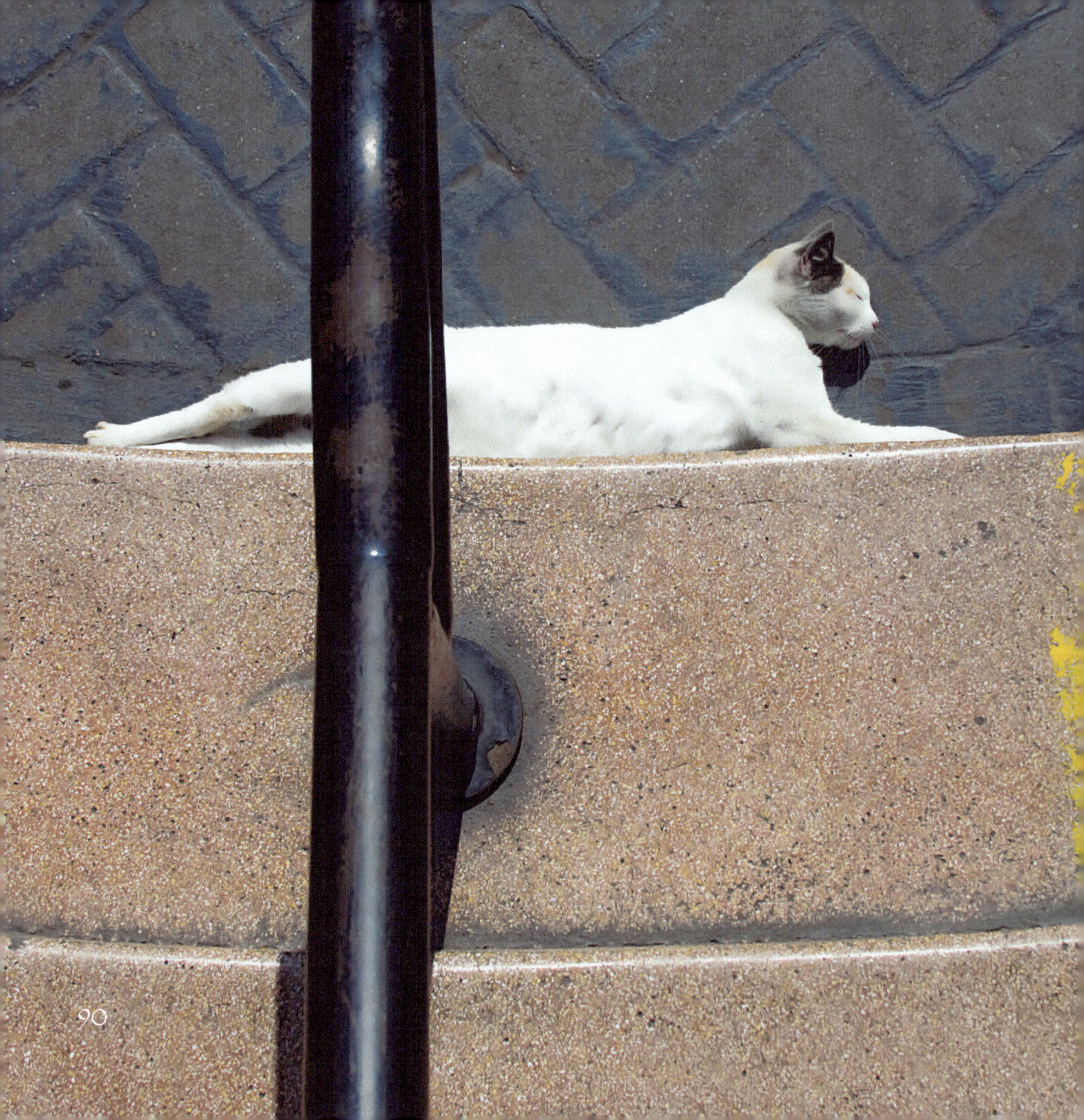

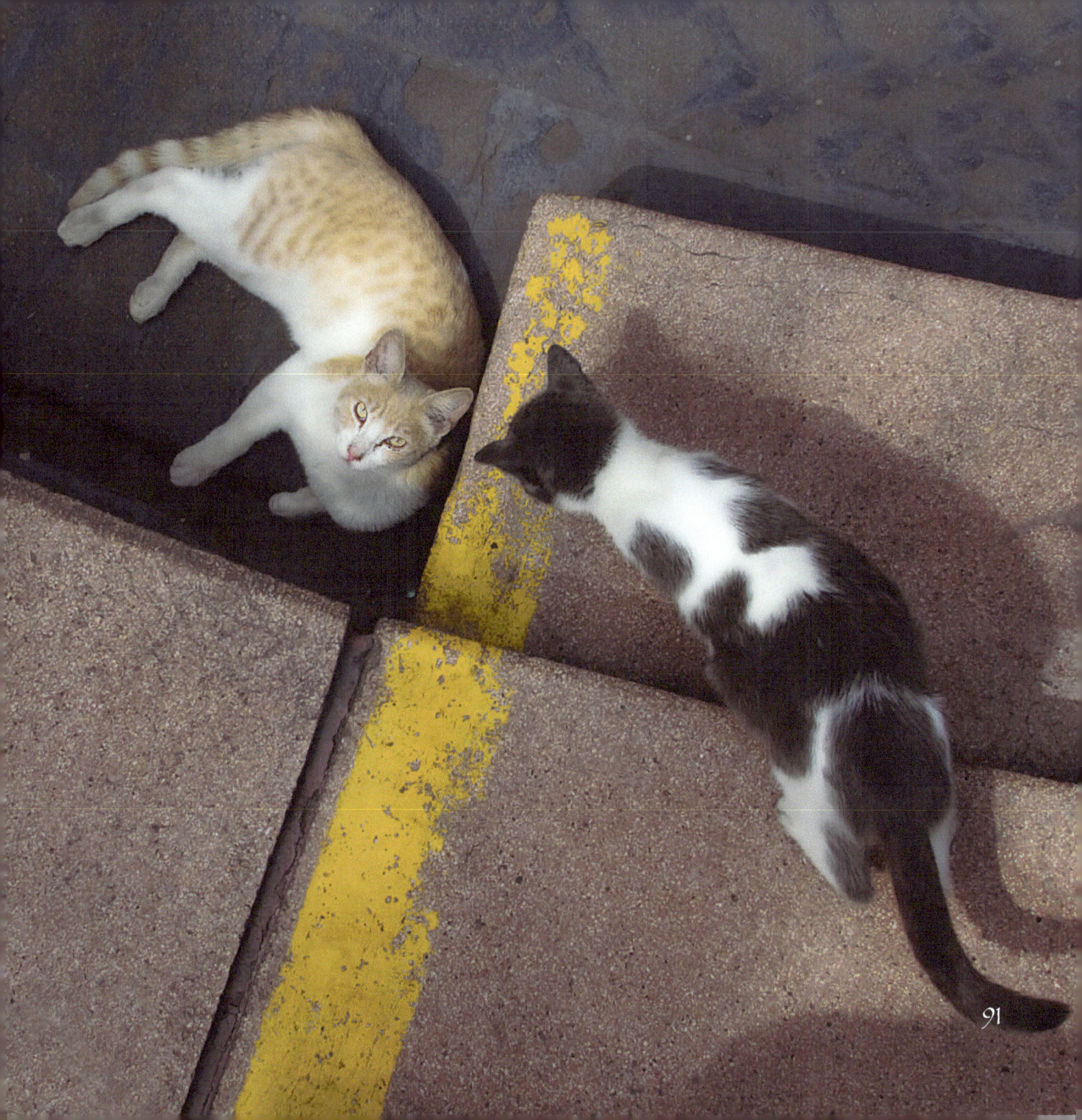

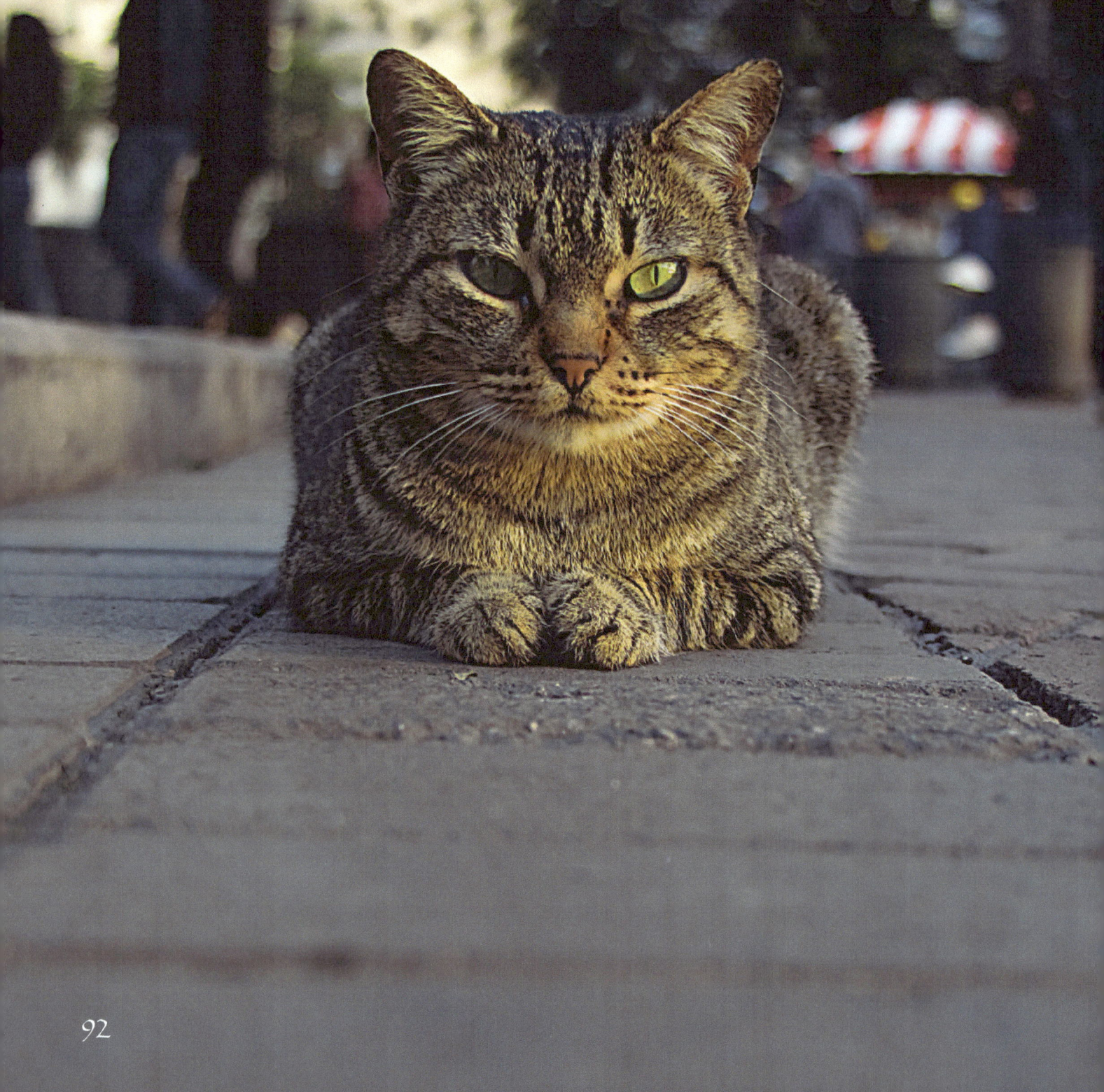

The Hotel Bolívar in Lima is famous for having invented the pisco sour

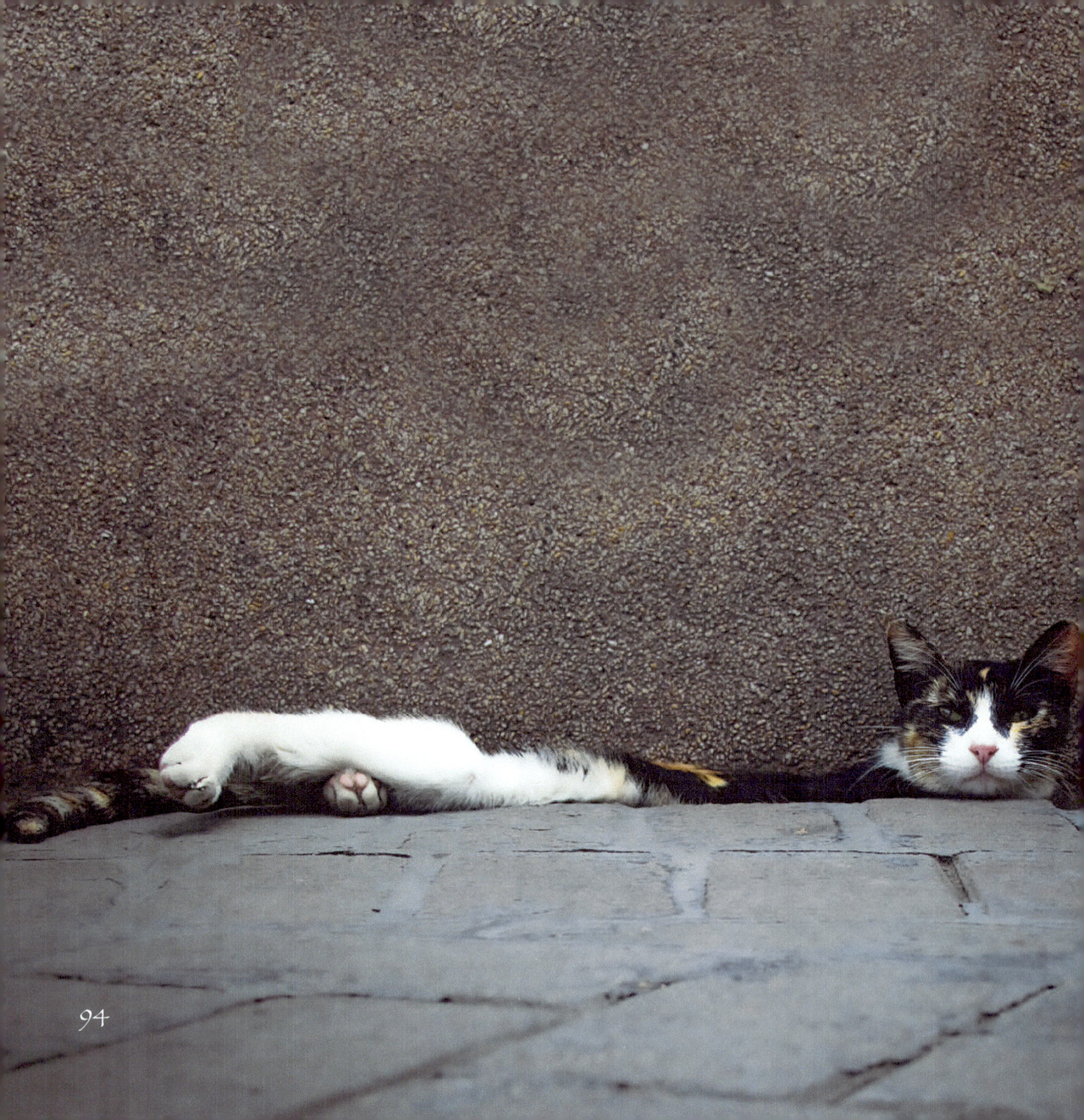

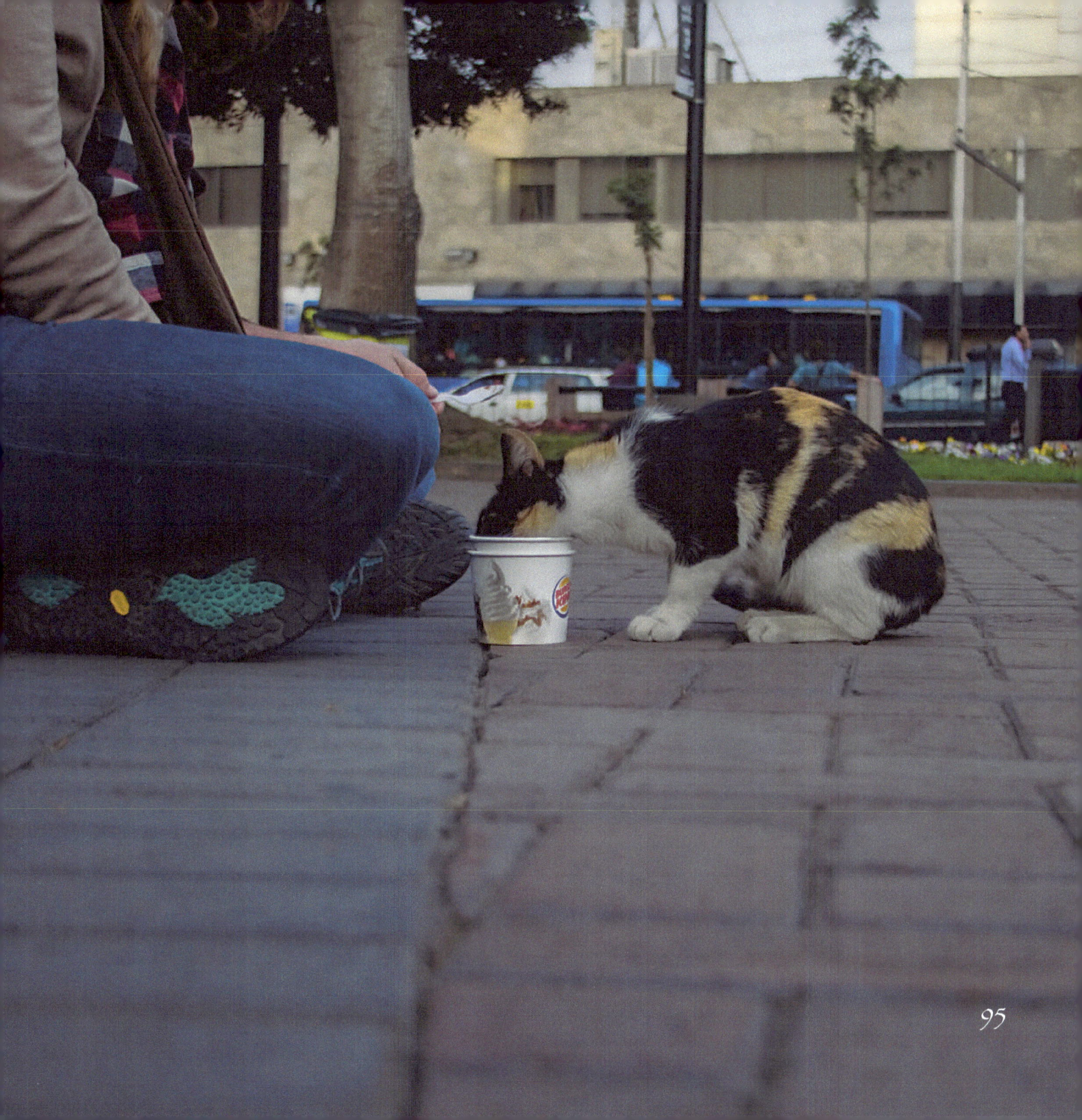

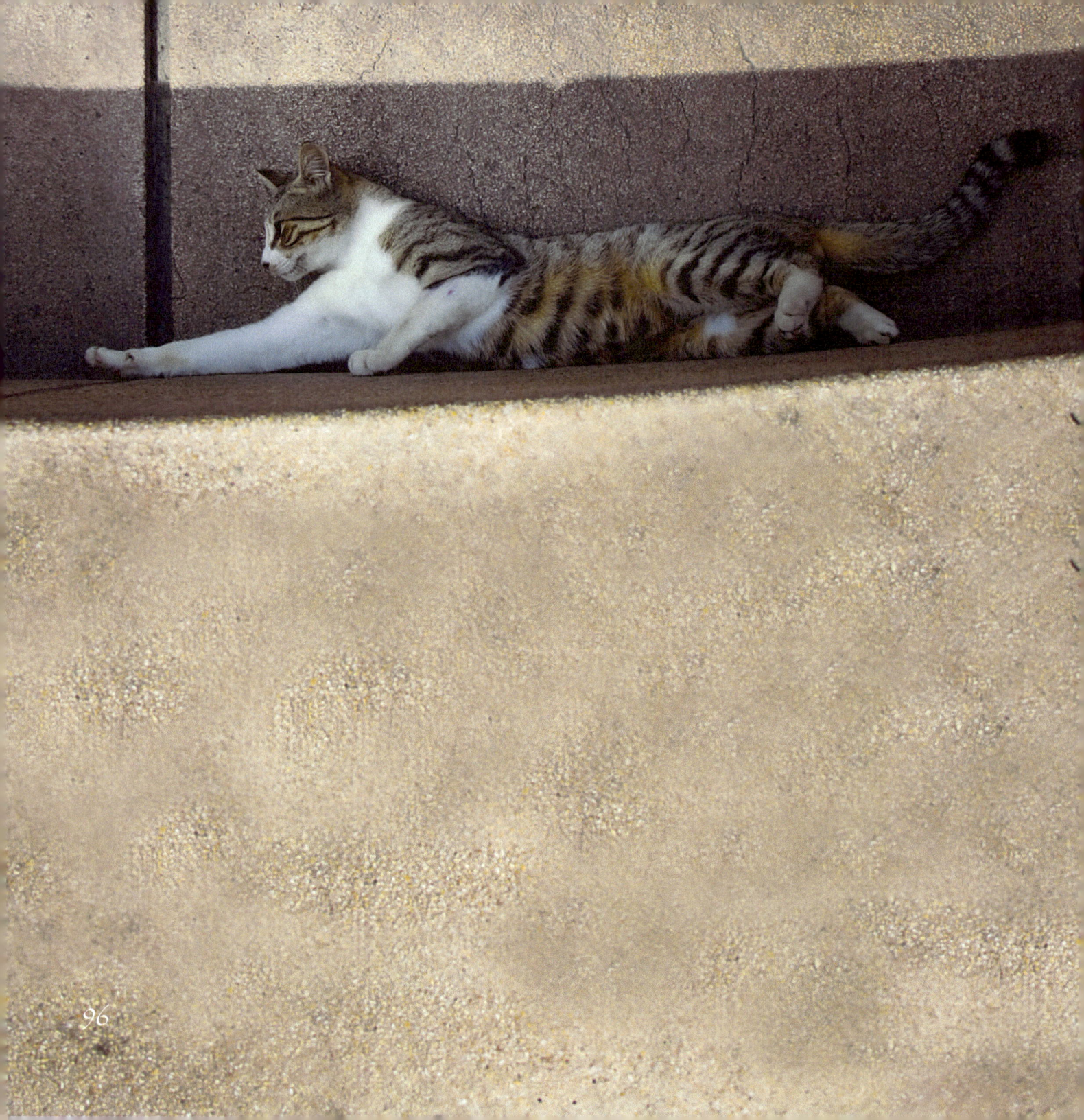

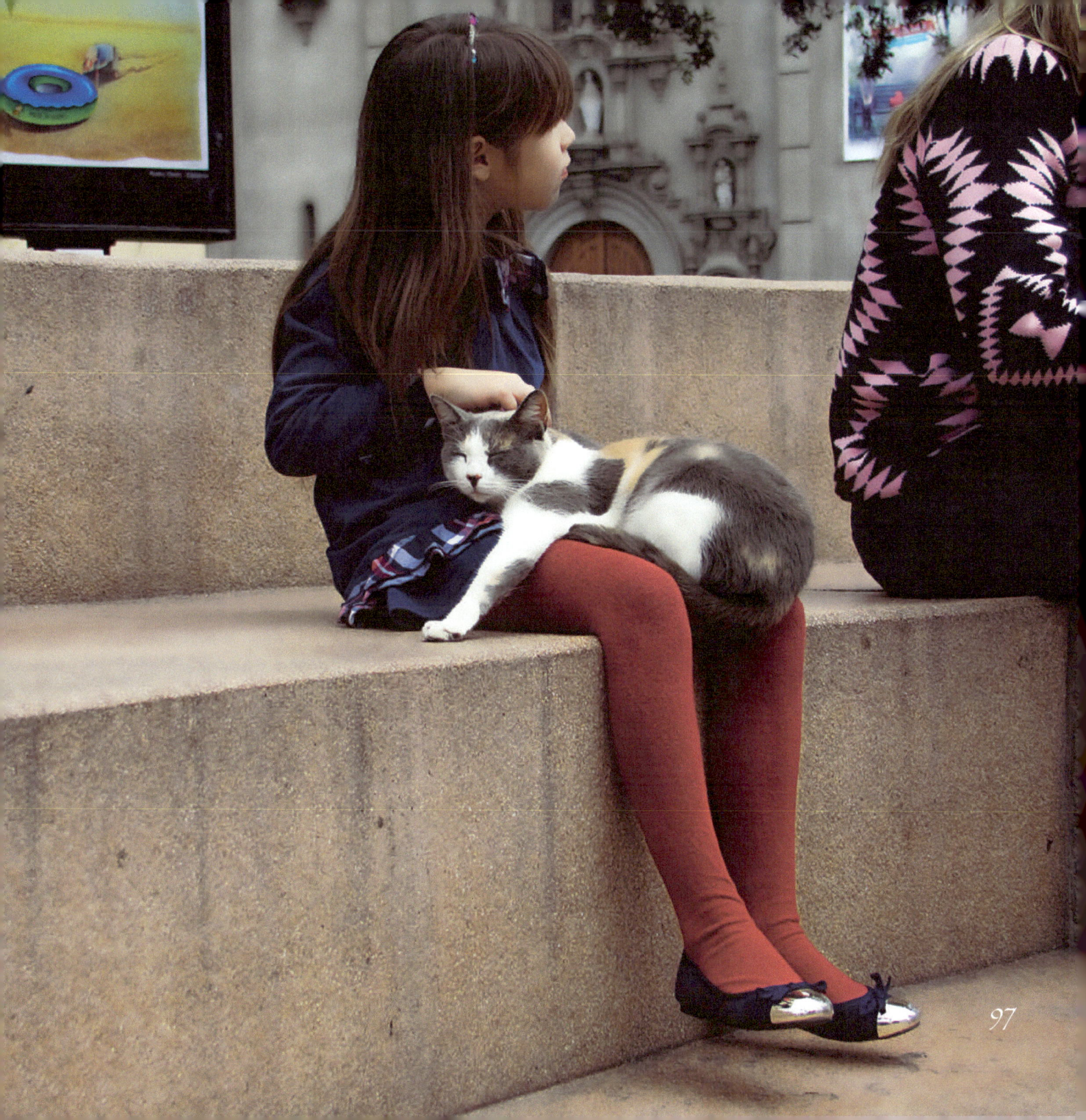

Almost 10% of a cat's bones are in its tail, which is used to maintain balance

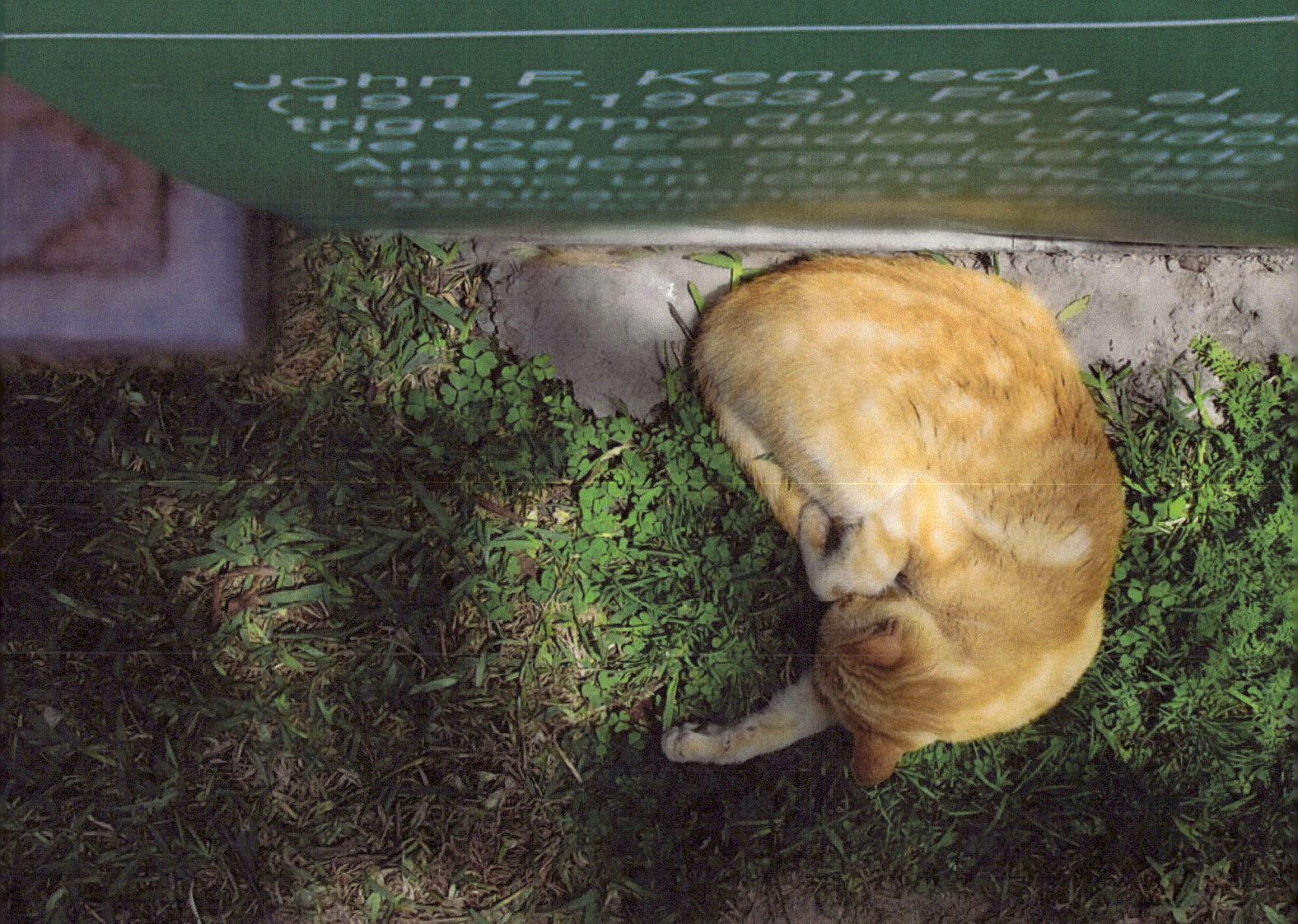

Parque John F. Kennedy

John F. Kennedy
(1917-1963): Fue el
trigésimo quinto presidente
de los Estados Unidos de
América, considerado
como un icono de las
aspiraciones estadounidenses

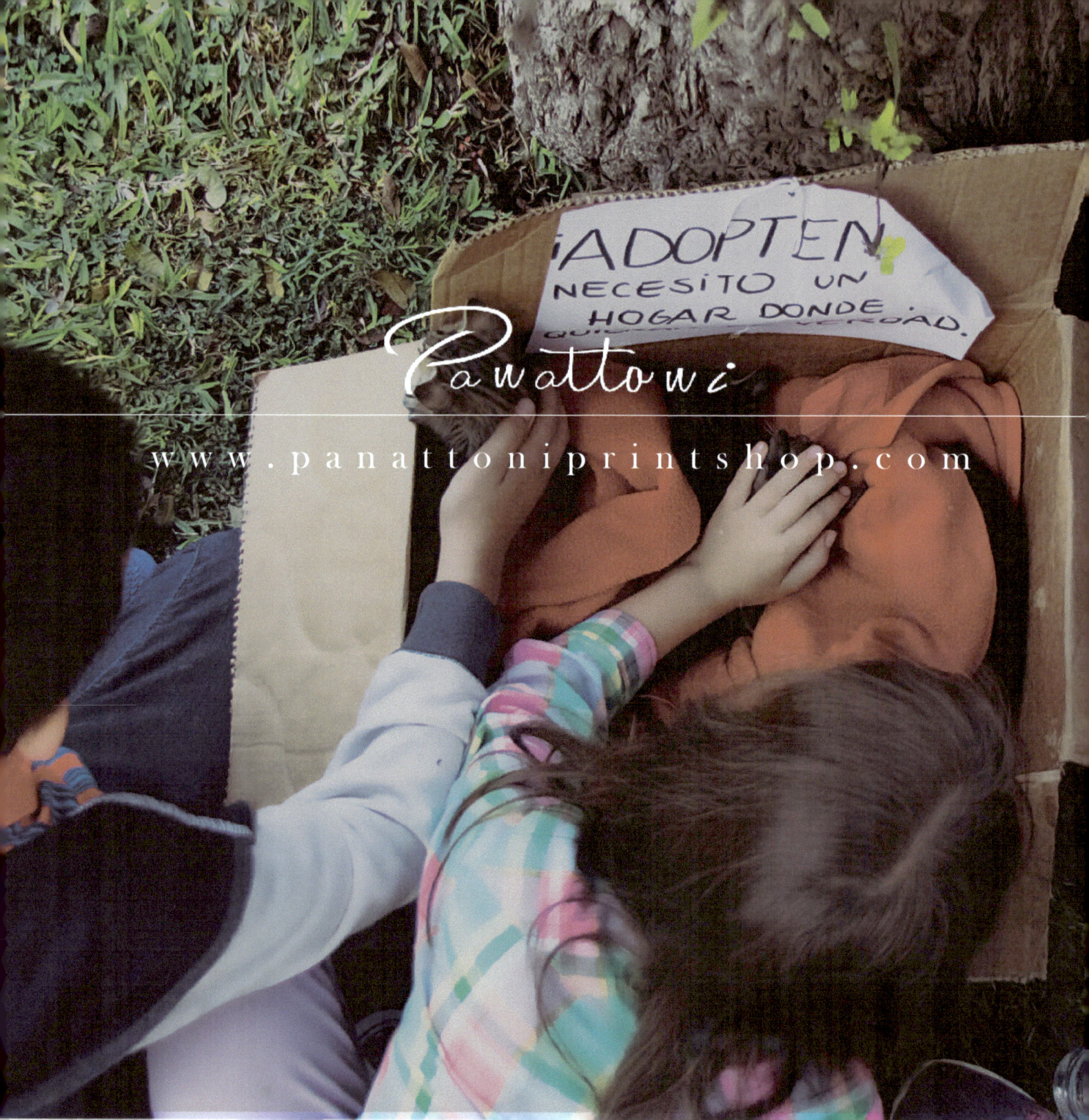

www.ingramcontent.com/pod-product-compliance
Lightning Source LLC
Chambersburg PA
CBHW040323190526
45162CB00007B/57